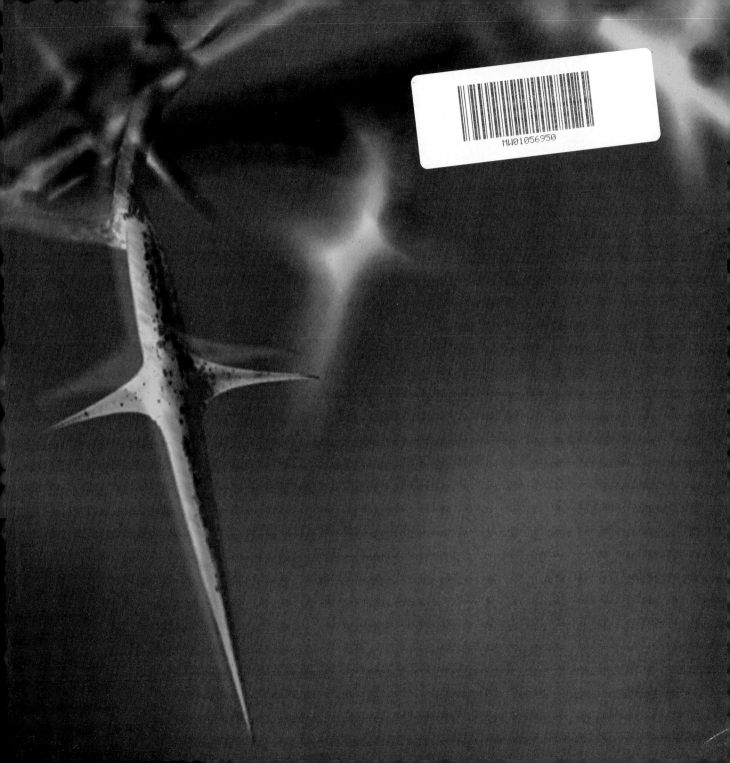

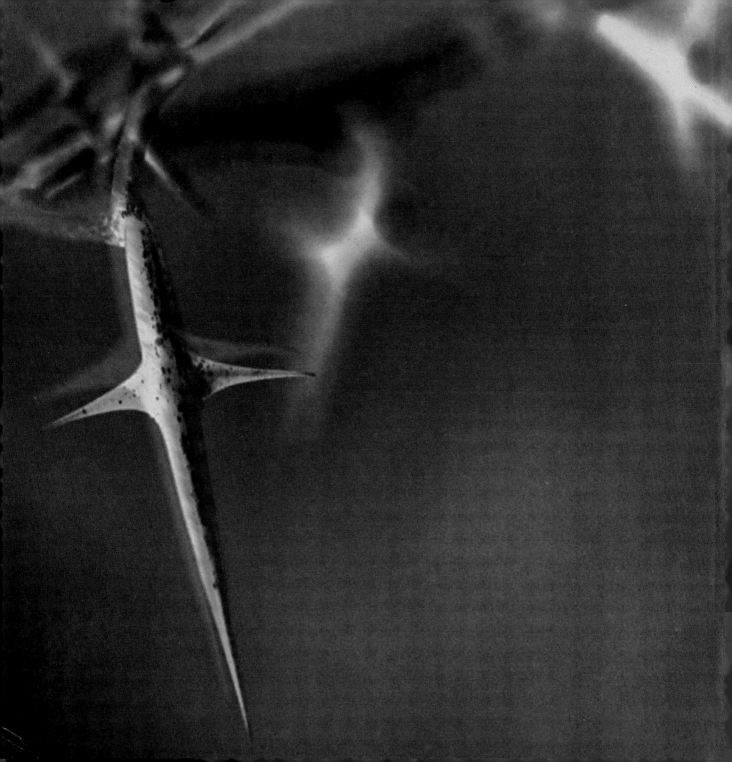

# ragamuffin prayers

COMPILED BY *Jimmy Abegg*

ccm

HARVEST HOUSE PUBLISHERS

RAGAMUFFIN PRAYERS
TEXT COPYRIGHT ©2000 BY JIMMY ABEGG
PUBLISHED BY HARVEST HOUSE PUBLISHERS
EUGENE, OREGON 97402 AND
CCM BOOKS, A DIVISION OF CCM COMMUNICATIONS
NASHVILLE, TENNESSEE 37205

LIBRARY OF CONGRESS CATALOGING-IN-PUBLICATION DATA
RAGAMUFFIN PRAYERS / COMPILED BY JIMMY ABEGG
P. CM.
ISBN 0-7369-0303-8
1. PRAYER–CHRISTIANITY. I. JIMMY A.

99-098000

BV210.2 .R24 2000
248.3'2–DC21

PRINTED IN THE UNITED STATES OF AMERICA.

HARVEST HOUSE PUBLISHERS  EUGENE, OREGON 97402

00 01 02 03 04 05 06 07 08 09 10 / BG / 10 9 8 7 6 5 4 3 2 1∎

R A G A M U F F I N   P R A Y E R S

# CONTENTS

## A LITTLE MIRACLE

If anything in this life beckons me to prayer and thanks, it would be these words spoken by Jesus of Nazareth: "Come to Me, all you who labor and are heavy laden, and I will give you rest. Take My yoke upon you, and learn from Me, for I am gentle and lowly in heart, and you will find rest for your souls" (Matthew 11:28,29 NKJV). I want to believe. I want relief from the moments of terror, when I think all my sins have finally caught up with me. Yet in the midst of life's struggles, I see miracles everywhere. And I've seen dreams become real.

This little book about prayer is one such miracle. It is the realization of a creative dream. I once told a girl I liked that I was working on a novel. She was quite impressed. Little did she know that I was flunking English! I wanted to write a book for her, but mostly I just wanted her to like me. It worked. I never had to show her my book. In fact, I never wrote a single word. I didn't think I could. Now I know that just making the effort is half the battle. Maybe someday I'll meet her again and give her a copy of this little book.

Some years after my stillborn "novel," I dreamed I could make photographs that told the truth about the world I lived in and expressed what I saw and felt about it. I began taking pictures of everything. Everywhere I went I took my camera and recorded what I saw. At about the same time, I first viewed the work of my friends Michael Wilson, Ben Pearson, Mark Tucker, and Frank Ockenfels. Their photographs taught me that taking pictures was more than a science. It was an art form, a way of revealing oneself and one's own vision.

This small miracle of a book is an opportunity to wed writing and the art of photography, to reveal something of what Jesus has done and is doing in my life and in the lives of other writers and artists.

I owe a debt of gratitude to a great many people for their role in making this book a reality: A special thanks to you, my friends who've contributed a bit of writing about what makes prayer meaningful to you. I know it was a challenge to try to share some of the mystery of how prayer works in your life. I appreciate the effort. Some of my most memorable moments as a person of faith have been in community with you all, and your gifts of transparency, vulnerability, reckless love, and ruthless enthusiasm have made my life as rich as anyone's I know. Thanks for sharing. I hope you find rest for your souls.

ACKNOWLEDGMENTS

A big hug to one of my best friends, Buddy Jackson, and to the people at Jackson Design. I've never seen a project in which so much was required in so short a time and yet was brought off so well. My heart is in your hands. Thanks, Karinne and Christie. Thanks also to Deb Rhodes for doing it again. And to Beth Lee, thanks for your help in getting it off the ground.

Since we could not have done this without the partnering and friendship of Terry Glaspey and Carolyn McCready at Harvest House Publishers, I want to say "this is just the beginning" and "thanks for going for it" all in the same breath. To Roberta Croteau at CCM, thanks for seeing it with me years ago!

To Tricia, Diana, Henry, Jim Chaffee, Chuck Nelson, and Mark and Karen Robinson: Thanks for friendship and support. Thanks to my wife Michelle and my daughters Alexia, Pierrette, and Jemina for not being easily impressed. AND MAY THE BLESSING OF MATTHEW 11 REST ON YOU, DEAR RAGAMUFFIN READER.

*Jimmy Abegg*

December 1999

RAGAMUFFINS KNOW THAT LIFE IS HARD, OFTEN FILLED WITH MUCH PAIN AND CONFUSION. BUT THEY ALSO KNOW THAT GOD IS FAITHFUL IN HIS LOVE. Rich Mullins was so taken by Manning's vision of the "Ragamuffin Gospel" that he named his band (of which I am a member) "A Ragamuffin Band." In his albums and concerts, Rich communicated passionately about the reckless and relentless "no strings attached" love of God. Though he was taken from us in a tragic car accident, Rich's legacy lives on, having an abiding influence on all the talented people who have contributed to this book. We have all come to understand that we are ragamuffins, much loved by God in the midst of all our shortcomings and failures. What you'll find in these pages is a candid glimpse at the hearts of some ragamuffins at prayer.

At its foundation, prayer is really a pretty simple thing, an instrument of communication between God and human beings. But what makes a book like this interesting is seeing that everyone plays on a slightly different instrument. In it we get a glimpse of the great variety in prayer. Some people need to be on their knees to pray, some people need to be in church, and others pray best in a place that is all their own—maybe sitting in their car in the garage with the music turned down low. Some people pray because they are in need. Others pray because they want the path to be easier for someone they love. Some pray for people who have passed away, in the hope that the suspicion they'll be reunited someday is in fact true. Some pray for people who aren't even born yet, like the mother who sends a prayer heavenward on behalf of the child that still waits in the womb or the husband and wife who pray for an empty womb to become fruitful. There are those whose prayers are almost entirely extemporized, made up on the spur of the moment in response to feelings and emotions, and others who like to pray from a set "menu," relying on the church's rich tradition of written prayers. How you pray is probably as unique as you are.

As a young man, eighteen years old, I participated in a five-week wilderness program called Outward Bound. I first had real contact with strong Christian believers through this program, out of which I arrived at one of the more unusual ways I have learned to pray. During what was called a "solo expedition"—three days alone in the Rocky Mountains of Colorado with only water, crackers, and some matches—I had my first moment of recognition regarding the condition of my heart. There in the middle of nowhere at 12,000 feet under starlit skies, I sat next to a fire I had built. I felt sure Jesus was speaking to me, calming my confused soul with a gentle and inviting voice of love. Since that time, at key junctures in my life, I've found it helpful to fast for the day, then go far out into the woods alone and build a fire. Then, sitting around the fire, I'll begin to pray. I know it's a pretty unusual practice, but I can't argue with its effectiveness. Several key chapters in my spiritual story followed times of conversation with God around a campfire. Prayer and fire are somehow connected in my mind, and I have had God speak to my heart in such settings.

Maybe it's because I'm a visual artist that I want to mark the importance of specific points in time. Or perhaps I'm like some Old Testament character piling up stones to build an altar in honor of a sacred moment. WHAT I KNOW IS THAT GOD MEETS ME THERE. OBVIOUSLY I CAN'T RUN TO THE WOODS EVERY TIME I NEED TO PRAY, BUT THIS PRACTICE REMINDS ME THAT I NEED TO MAKE ROOM IN MY LIFE FOR PRAYER.

One of the most powerful ways I've learned to pray is what the classic writer Brother Lawrence called "the practice of the presence of God." It comes from learning to make yourself cognizant of God's presence in your life, remembering that you are always living out your life in awareness of the fact that God is with you. Life itself becomes a prayer. But living a life of prayer is difficult, a mystery that continues to unfold for me.

I am learning that prayer is more than just an obligation. Sometimes we can be swayed by the idea that there is some certain way to pray and an expectation for how much you do it. We can suffer from feeling that we have failed to live up to some sort of standard. But what God wants most is honesty, for us to open our hearts and come to Him without pretense or posturing. Some of my most powerful prayers aren't even couched in "proper" language. MANY OF THEM I WOULDN'T DARE PRAY ALOUD IN CHURCH. BUT THEY ARE HONEST CRIES FROM MY HEART. SOMETIMES THE BEST PRAYERS ARE SOMETHING LIKE THIS: "OH MY GOD, HELP." I think one of the fundamental requirements of an authentic prayer is passion, to come before Him with all your heart and lay it all on the line.

# The Lords Prayer

Our Father, who art in heaven,
Hallowed be thy Name.
Thy Kingdom come, Thy will
be done, On earth as it
is in heaven. Give us this
day our daily bread. And
forgive us our trespasses, As
we forgive those who trespass
against us. And lead us not
into temptation, but deliver us
from evil. For thine is the
Kingdom, and the power, and
the glory, for ever and ever. Amen

*Jimmy Abegg*

The book you are holding in your hands is about prayer. In these pages you'll find some profound reflections on what it means to pray and some beautiful examples of prayer at work. But this is not the place to look for the "last word" on the subject—I don't think any of the contributors would consider themselves to be experts on prayer. We are just a group of people who have learned something about prayer through practicing it.

The uniqueness of this particular book is probably to be found in its perspective. What these writers share in common, other than a common faith in Christ, is the realization that we can never live up to the demands of religious perfectionism that many Christians aspire toward as their goal. Instead, we know that we are imperfect, frail, and fallen people. We are "ragamuffins." As far as I know, it was Brennan Manning who first coined this word to describe the spiritual state of the one who knows that he or she is deeply loved by God as a simple gift of God's grace. As he wrote in *Lion and Lamb: The Relentless Tenderness of Jesus:*

> *God's love is based on nothing, and the fact that it is based on nothing makes us secure. Were it based on anything we do, and that anything were to collapse, then God's love would crumble as well. But with the God of Jesus no such thing can possibly happen. People who realize this can live freely and to the fullest.*

My hope in this book is to expose you to a wide variety of perspectives on prayer, letting the common threads emerge as you read these essays, prayers, and poems from some of the friends I've made along my own journey. They fit together like a quilt constructed of faith, hope, and love. I've also included some of my photographs. Some of these photos celebrate the majesty and glory of God's creation or mark places that have struck me as particularly "holy"— places where God's presence can be seen and felt. Others serve as a reminder that God's hand can be recognized in even the small and ordinary things of our lives. Either way, they bear witness to the awesomeness and the mystery of God. Perhaps the photos themselves will be a catalyst to prayer.

I've enjoyed partnering with many different sorts of people on various kinds of creative projects over the years. I am so thankful for such opportunities as this one. If not for the generosity of many friends who agreed to contribute their thoughts on the subject of prayer, this book could never have become what it is: Not just an exercise in "art for art's sake," but a collection of honest, soul-searching, and beautiful meditations. I thank each friend and contributor, and pray that God would wrap each in the warm embrace of His love as He continues to reveal Himself in their prayers. And may you, reader, experience the same thing as you read and look and join in the journey we make to find more room in our hearts for Christ. WE ARE RAGAMUFFINS ALL. ✸

*Carolyn Arends*

The relatives on my father's side were farmers—hard working, plain spoken people who understood and loved the earth and harnessed its power throughout sweat and skill and faith. At least that is how I imagine them. I am prone to remember them in fits of romantic contemplation, during which I suspect something of their noble, earthy spirit lives on in me. In my more lucid moments I see, clearly, it does not. I am the poster girl for comfort-craving city dwellers everywhere, and when I get close to the earth I so profess to love, it seems, well…dirty.

I was not without promise in my early childhood. No Fisher Price farm set was ever as beloved as mine, and for six futile birthdays in a row I asked passionately and expectantly for a pony, whom I planned to call "Black Beauty" and keep in my bedroom. I see further evidence of my proud ancestry in my son, who at eighteen months is so enamored with cows that he reaches heights of near ecstasy in the dairy section of our local supermarket. "Moo!" he cries, oblivious to the chill, pointing to the pastoral scenes that adorn each and every milk carton with a fervor that would have made his great-grandma Bittner most pleased.

I met my great-grandmother Bittner only once, when I was very young. My parents, in a sudden spasm of suburban guilt (at least I know where I get it from), decided it was time to embark on a pilgrimage to the family homestead. And so, in the summer of 1972, my brother Chris and I spent a wide-eyed week on the Bittner wheat farm in Yorktown, Saskatchewan.

A FOUR-YEAR-OLD POSSESSES A MIND'S EYE LIKE A FUN HOUSE MIRROR—THE SHAPES OF EVERYONE AND EVERYTHING ARE STRETCHED TO LARGER-THAN-LIFE PROPORTIONS. TO THIS DAY I CAN PLAY BACK MY MEMORIES LIKE SCRATCHY PIECES OF SLOW-MOTION FILM.

The wheat is militant, standing at attention in uniform rows until a prairie wind spots me in the distance and decides to put on a show. Stalks higher than the Empire State Building become Motown dancers, bending and swaying, swaying and bending for an awestruck audience of one. My great-uncles are benevolent Goliaths with wide grins and huge, leathery hands. At the end of the day they smell a little like ripe fruit. Their own children are no longer children, yet when they enter the farmhouse they are once more the dutiful sons of Grandma Bittner, who is all one could hope for in a family matriarch. Eighty-five laborious years have compromised her mobility (I picture her in a wheel chair— my parents tell me it was really just a kitchen chair from which she seldom moved), but she is still a dominant figure. I am a little afraid in her presence, but there is a softness beneath her severe strength. The Saskatchewan sun has turned her golden brown, and she is as kneaded and plump as the fragrant loaves of bread cooling on her counters.

The Bittner wheat farm is pure magic, but I am not purely happy. Even a four-year-old can tell when something is amiss, and I am troubled when my uncles' open faces cloud over. I strain to overhear and understand their conversations. The crops are in trouble. No rain for months. We hoist Grandma Bittner into the car for a drive, and each field we pass elicits the same response. Too dry, too dry. My heart sinks further with every mournful shake of her heavy head. I've never heard the word "drought" before, but I'm sure it's not good.

In the cool of the evening my great-aunts and uncles gather in the kitchen and bring my parents up to date on the latest family gossip. Chris and I grow restless, so one night we are permitted to sit by ourselves on the front porch. We are sleepy and warm and somewhat intoxicated with our freedom, until all at once the universe begins to go horribly wrong.

A cloud of mosquitoes attacks my brother. The air is thick with them, and they only want Chris. We are both hysterical, and the grown-ups come running in the kind of panic that leaves spilt teacups and crushed pastries in its wake. The family surrounds my brother, and he is as frightened by their flailing attempts to beat off the insects as he is by the mosquitoes themselves. Eventually they manage to get him inside, and the surviving mosquitoes fly away in a well-fed stupor. With the resiliency only a two-year-old can possess, Chris is happy once again, consoled by some chocolate and an ancient set of building blocks.

Now I am alone on the porch, still sweaty and jittery from my brother's ordeal. Before my heart rate can return to normal, a new onslaught is launched. But this time it is not mosquitoes.

The world is suddenly lit in a ghoulish white flash. A second later, all is consumed in darkness. The wind begins to howl, enraged to be losing this shouting match with a thunder that is more terrifying than anything I've ever heard or imagined. The rain the heavens have been hoarding is released with a savage vengeance, pelting the roof and slashing at the windows, drenching me instantly. Even the sturdy old farmhouse has turned against me, violently banging the screen door open and shut behind me. The lightning strikes again and again and again, illuminating the holy terror that is my first prairie storm.

My parents find me inside the farmhouse, sitting on the cellar stairs, my hands clamped over my ears in an effort to drown out the rattle of the rain crashing into the huge metal rain-water cistern next to me. I am nearly doubled over by my sobs. My father scoops me up and carries me into safety of the kitchen. A flash of hot light illuminates my relatives for a moment. They are sitting together staring out the farmhouse windows with inexplicably calm smiles. "It's just a storm," they murmur. There is even some quiet, gentle laughter. I only cry harder.

"Sweetheart," pleads my mom, "don't be afraid." I shake my head. I am afraid, but more than that I am sick with guilt so crushing I can't speak under the weight of it. The family—both immediate and extended—is sympathetic, patient. They don't understand that the chaos outside is all my fault. "What is it? What is it?" they chorus.

Several minutes pass before I summon the courage to confess my terrible secret.

I...PRAYED...FOR...RAIN.

Now the laughter is not so quiet. There is even a little applause. "Oh, Honey, the rain is wonderful," someone says. Before I can catch my breath the uncles are teasing me. Someone brings me some warm milk, and soon I can't keep my heavy eyes open, not even to watch the storm. "Hey Sweetheart," calls an uncle as my daddy carries me off to my room, "Could you pray for some cash?"

In the morning I awake to the sound of my uncles' hammers. They are repairing wind-damaged fences, and they are still laughing, jubilant in the mud. The crops will make it after all.

The storm and the terror, the giddy relief and elation, the instinctual and unwavering belief that my prayers had saved the Bittner family farm—these are among my earliest memories. And I consider them now with a sense of wonder and dread that has only deepened over the years. The night the drought of '72 came to an end, I began to understand that there are forces even towering great—uncles cannot tame, forces so ferocious in their power that—even if they bring you exactly what you need (especially if they bring you exactly what you need)—they are likely to scare you silly. I had already heard much about God in my young life—already, I think, learned to love Him. But hearing the heavens thunder, I had my first taste of what it is to fear Him, my first encounter with what a quarter of a century later I am learning to call the *mysterium tremendum et fascinans*—the tremendous and fascinating mystery of God. On the front steps of that Yorktown farmhouse, a holy secret was whispered into my soul: Prayer is the point of access, the place where the finite and the infinite intersect and converse. To pray is to enter at least a little ways into the mystery, or—and this is even more dangerous—to invite the mystery to come to you.

I have prayed every day of the last twenty-seven years, and yet it is only lately that I have become enough of a disciple to begin to study prayer—to stand with the others and say, "Lord, teach me to pray." I recently devoured Richard Foster's incredible book *Prayer: Finding the Heart's True Home*, startled to discover how many kinds of prayer are part of the Christian tradition: The Prayer of the Forsaken, The Prayer of Tears, The Prayer of Relinquishment, Meditative Prayer, Contemplative Prayer, Petitionary Prayer, Intercessory Prayer, and a dozen more. I have prayed many types of prayers throughout my life, but my haphazard list is quite different from Foster's.

I have been a specialist in the "Let's Make A Deal" school of prayer: *If You will only let me pass this test* (for which I have not read the textbook), *I will spend the rest of my life earnestly studying in a convent.* My years of frequent travel have also honed my "Turbulence Prayers." Typically whispered on airplanes that appear destined to crash, these prayers focus upon achieving meet-my-Maker readiness: *God, if there's anything not right between us, I confess it now.* I can also claim extensive experience with "Futility Prayers," prayers that seldom work, but are prayed passionately anyway. *Please make my newborn sleep through at least part of the night* is one Futility Prayer. Another is: *Please don't let me throw up.*

However theologically incorrect my prayers may be, I have discovered that whatever is in my heart must be either prayed out or left to fester. And so I dare to utter my petty, self-interested requests, trusting—praying—that the Holy Spirit will intercede on my behalf with groans my words (or lack thereof) cannot express, translating my impetuous, childish gibberish into communion with God.

When I read that if I ask God for bread He will not give me a stone, I realize that He not only desires to give me what I need, He wants me to come ask Him for it. This to me is the greatest miracle, the deeper mystery—the God of the Universe wants me to speak with Him. Heaven knows I am not a great conversationalist—I talk too much, listen too little—but He desires my company anyway.

There is so much I want to learn about prayer. CAN OUR REQUESTS CHANGE THE COURSE OF HISTORY? CAN WE CHANGE THE MIND AND WILL OF GOD? ARE THE HAND OF FATE AND THE HAND OF GOD LOCKED IN SOME SORT OF WRESTLING MATCH THAT HINGES ON OUR PETITIONS? I have received certain and dramatic answers to some of my prayers. To others I have been able to perceive nothing but the deafening roar of silence. In some cases I have eventually discovered why my prayers were answered with a "no" or a "not yet." In many others I remain bewildered. But I will study the Scriptures and I will wait on the Lord and I am hopeful that more will be revealed. Regardless, I will pray, because understanding follows obedience, and because my life would not be worth living if I could not cry out to the God who gave it to me.

However uncertain I am about the way prayer changes the unfolding of events, I have been shown clearly that prayer changes me. When I begin to pray for an enemy, my heart like a fist clenched with anger, I am opened up until I can no longer hold the resentment and frustration. When I plead with the Publican, "Lord, have mercy on me, a sinner," I travel a little deeper into the mercy of God. When I confess with the Centurion, "I believe, help my unbelief," my faith is made a little stronger.

And so I pray. Whether I am praying from a surrendered or a stubborn heart, I speak with the God of Creation. I am ushered, sometimes reverent, sometimes willful, never worthy, into His presence. When the language is beyond me, it is spoken on my behalf. I pray for the wisdom to learn more about prayer, and for the courage to pray the prayers that will change me. AND IN MY BEST AND BRAVEST MOMENTS, WHEN I ACHE TO KNOW MORE OF THE TREMENDOUS AND FASCINATING MYSTERY OF GOD, I PRAY FOR RAIN. ✺

## PRAYERS FROM THE EDGE

Like Amelia Earhart looking for Howland Island.
"Mayday...low on fuel...can't see."
Breath short, knuckles clutching.
The world has the crystalline patina of panic in black and white.
"Help me."
One would gather God retains the option.

## PRAYERS FROM HOME

One day life stops making sense.
You have an appointment at the children's cemetery, for instance.
The little headstone reads "Our Sissy."
The math is simple. She would have been five this year.
The world rendered all shadow and bent rays.
"Who do I see about this?"

## PRAYERS FROM A PENLIGHT

You look up one summer night
And see the billion burning suns of the Milky Way.
You've been informed this is barely a drop in the cosmic ocean,
So you snap a self−portrait, all hair and glasses and dental work,
And hold it up to the sky.
"KNOW ME."

## PRAYERS FROM SLEEP

Just the sound of your own breathing now.
Each exhale bears a sigh.
Followed by silence, an epic crisis.
You have no claim on what happens next.
Yours only to be filled.
To be the instrument of a holy rhythm.

PRAYERBOOK *Billy Crockett*

I wish I could say I was a mighty prayer warrior, an exemplary man of prayer who could offer life-changing insights into the art of prayer. But I can't. In fact, praying is one of the most difficult areas of my life. I don't pray nearly as much as I know I should. Truth is, it isn't always easy to find the time to pray. When I get out of bed in the morning, I am often overwhelmed by all the duties and responsibilities pulling me in so many different directions: my family, my work, the phone calls, the interviews, the various demands that people make on my time. Life doesn't slow down and wait for you to catch up. It just keeps moving on. Suddenly you find yourself sitting in the middle of all the chaos asking yourself, "What am I doing?" You realize you've lost touch, that you're stuck in the rat race. When this happens to me I am reminded how much I need the peaceful presence of God in my life. Sometimes the most healing kind of prayer is just sitting still in the presence of God, being quiet enough to listen to Him.

I believe in the power of prayer. I've seen it work in the lives of others, and I've seen it work in my own life. My life has been filled with many miracles, both big and small. One of the most amazing answers to prayer I ever experienced was when my wife, Deb, couldn't get pregnant. We had given up hope of having children. In fact, the doctor told us that Deb would never have kids. Well, we went to our pastor, Don Finto, and asked him if he thought we should go for further tests at Vanderbilt University Hospital and check into their program for this problem. "Yeah," he said, "that would be fine, but before you do that, let's anoint you guys with oil and pray for you." So they did just that. The elders gathered to pray for the Lord to open her womb. Four months later she was pregnant with the first of our five children. I eventually had to call our pastor and ask him to take us off the prayer list! Witnessing our success, a number of other couples went to the elders for prayer and conceived for the first time. Prayer works!

I've never taken prayer lightly. I've never prayed to the Lord to help me be successful or famous or to sell a lot of records. I've never asked God to make me creative. These aren't the things that matter most to me.

My prayers are ragamuffin prayers. They are not carefully crafted religious petitions as much as they are prayers arising out of my neediness and wonderment at God's amazing love. When it comes right down to it, I'm not sure there is any other kind of prayer than a ragamuffin prayer. God doesn't demand polish and precision from our prayers. He wants honesty from our hearts. We'll never be able to be good enough to deserve to be heard. We are desperate people, in dire need of a God who loves us. Only through the love and power of Christ am I empowered to lift my voice in prayer.

My own prayers are very conversational. I speak with God as with the dearest of friends, as someone who really knows me and really understands the struggles of my life. I find I am expressing myself as though He is right there with me. Which, of course, He is. So I open my heart without a lot of pretense. "You know, Lord, I said this the other day, but You know what I'm feeling..." My prayers are so personal that sometimes I feel uncomfortable praying in front of an audience. But the amazing thing is that sometimes someone will come up to me afterwards and say, "Man, I've never heard anybody pray like that..." CHRISTIANS SOMETIMES THINK THAT PRAYERS HAVE TO BE PROFOUND AND WELL ARTICULATED TO BE ACCEPTABLE TO GOD. BUT IT'S GREAT TO KNOW THAT WE CAN BARE OUR HEART IN RAGGED HONESTY BEFORE THE LORD. WHICH IS WHAT I TRY TO DO.

Here's what I pray for: I pray for God to draw me closer to Him, to invade my life with His presence.

I pray for my family, for my wife and my kids. These are probably some of my most passionate prayers. I pray that God will keep them safe. That He will guide and protect them, that they will know His love. Next to my relationship with God and with my wife, my kids are my number one priority. If God were to ask me what one prayer I'd like to have answered, it would be this: That my kids would grow up to love and fear the Lord. I want them to become God lovers!

I pray prayers of thanksgiving for how God has used me. I don't deserve to be used as powerfully as God has used my life and talents. Sometimes I pray "Wow! Why me? But thank You!" I am amazed at what God can accomplish despite my weaknesses.

I pray prayers of thanks for the small beauties of life. One day several years ago, I was driving through town when I turned off on an unfamiliar side street. I can't remember exactly what errand I was on, but suddenly I saw these incredibly beautiful pear trees. They were in full bloom, unspeakably gorgeous. I pulled up alongside the trees and just sat there and took in their beauty. Suddenly my eyes filled with tears. I sat there and cried for five minutes, sobbing and praying, "Thank You, Lord. Thank You." It made me think about how many times I have missed such precious small gifts from the Lord. Sometimes it is the little stuff for which we should be most thankful. To me those tears were the purest form of the prayer of thanksgiving.

Finally I pray the prayer that is in the last book of the Bible: "Lord Jesus, come quickly." There is so much still to be done in the world, so much pain and hurt and injustice to be healed and set right. And only the coming of His kingdom will really bring us peace. ONLY HE CAN RESCUE RAGAMUFFINS LIKE YOU AND ME. ✺

`atlantic ocean`          Dingle , Republic of Ireland 1997

I wish I could say that my prayer life is completely consistent and without flaw. But since I am neither, it would be untrue to say that my prayers are. Truth is, I am driven by extremes. When I am very up or very down, my communication with the Father is amazing. He knows me very well because my life has been full of both extremes!

When God made me, I believe He made a roller coaster with my name on it at the same time. He saw my heart and said, "I know what this kid needs." The click, click, clicking sound of that first big hill woke me in the womb and continues to wake me every day.

Each morning, I get out of bed and commit to keep my arms and legs inside the ride at all times. I ask God to carry me through the laughs and screams, the exhilaration and the horror that I know from experience is awaiting me.

Each evening, I climb out exhausted and thrilled to have completed the ride one more time. I sleep in peace, knowing tomorrow I'll get back on the ride…my ride. Locked into place, I'll throw my hands in the air, feel the wind in my face, and trust. I will trust the One who designed both me and the ride to take me through the ups and downs, round and round one more time. It's what I need. It's what I want. And I'm so glad He knows me so well. ✹

"MAY ALL YOUR EXPECTATIONS
BE FRUSTRATED.
MAY ALL YOUR PLANS BE THWARTED.
MAY ALL OF YOUR DESIRES
BE WITHERED INTO NOTHINGNESS,
THAT YOU MAY EXPERIENCE THE POWERLESSNESS AND
POVERTY OF A CHILD AND SING AND DANCE
IN THE LOVE OF GOD THE FATHER,
THE SON AND THE SPIRIT."

BLESSING GIVEN TO HENRI NOUWEN BY HIS SPIRITUAL MENTOR

A TERRIBLE PRAYER *Michael Yaconelli*

I HAVE ALWAYS BEEN TERRIBLE AT PRAYING.

I FORGET.

MY MIND WANDERS.

I FALL ASLEEP.

I DON'T PRAY ENOUGH.

I DON'T UNDERSTAND WHAT PRAYER IS

OR WHAT PRAYER DOES.


IF PRAYER WERE SCHOOL...

I WOULD FLUNK PRAYING.


BUT PRAYER ISN'T SCHOOL.

IT IS MYSTERY.


MAYBE THE MYSTERY IS...

JESUS LOVES TERRIBLE PRAYERS.

MAYBE...

WHEN I CAN'T THINK OF ANYTHING TO SAY, HE SAYS WHAT I CAN'T SAY.

WHEN I TALK TOO MUCH, HE CHERISHES MY TOO—MANY WORDS.

WHEN I FALL ASLEEP, HE HOLDS ME IN HIS LAP AND CARESSES MY WEARY SOUL.

WHEN I AM OVERWHELMED WITH GUILT AT MY INCONSISTENT, INADEQUATE PRAYING

HE WHISPERS, "YOUR NAME IS ALWAYS ON MY LIPS."


I AM FILLED WITH GRATITUDE, MY SOUL OVERFLOWS WITH THANKFULNESS AND I...

I...FIND MYSELF SAYING OVER AND OVER AGAIN, "THANK YOU."

PRAYING THE MYSTERY.

❀

Sometimes there is a thin line between superstition and spiritual discipline—between those who take the Lord's name in vain and those who speak it as a cry for help. "Oh, my God!" is a phrase that we hear fairly frequently. In its brevity and abruptness, the blasphemy of a careless soul can sometimes sound a little like the heartfelt cry of a ragamuffin. There are moments when the best we can muster in our response to tragedy is something along the lines of "Oh, my God!" Perhaps we cannot find the strength within to articulate our need at that exact moment and such an almost wordless cry is the best we can muster.

I grew up in Ballymena, County Antrim in the northern part of Ireland. The northern counties are to Ireland what the southern states are to America—the Bible Belt. It is a culture that stresses holiness and righteousness, focusing a great deal of attention on the rules and regulations by which a Christian should live. And despite the best intentions, these regulations, once meant to spur one toward holiness, often harden into a legalism not unlike that of the Pharisees. The name of the Lord is very much protected and respected. And this is, I suppose, the way it ought to be. When I hear someone utter "Jesus Christ" or "Oh my God," a shudder rushes up my spine. My sin radar sends bright sulphurous flashes across my soul.

Thirty years into my life and thirteen into my Christian pilgrimage, I moved to Dublin in the Republic of Ireland. I soon discovered that I had moved from a predominantly Protestant culture to one shaped by many years of Catholicism. Among the many adjustments I had to make was in responding to the different attitude to the Divine name. It was not uncommon to hear people use the names of God and Jesus in their daily shouts of wonder and cries of struggle.

So even now, five years after my Dublin sojourn, I'm wondering if these shouts and cries could be ragamuffin prayers—genuine calls to God in praise and pleading.

Undoubtedly they are sometimes just thoughtless blasphemy. But could they, at other times, be sincere attempts at connecting with God in the midst of everyday events of life? This way of connecting harkens back to the Celtic Christianity of Ireland's past, where blessings and prayers were threaded into every chore, every meeting, every part of the daily routine.

I have recently been talking with my good friend Timothy Flaherty, an Irish speaker (very rare among Protestants) currently studying for a master's degree in Irish at the University of Ulster focused on Gaelic greetings. Such a course of study is unheard of among Protestants. His feedback has been very interesting. He tells me that if you meet someone on the roads of the Gaeltacht, instead of saying "hello" you would say "Dia duit" (God save you). The proper reply would be "Dia is Muire duit" (God and Mary save you). Blessings like these are an important part of the everyday greetings and sayings in traditional Irish culture. Entering a house you would declare, "Dia sa teach" (God in the house). Upon leaving you would say, "Beannacht leat" (blessings with you) or "Go dtuga Dia slán abhaile tú" (May God give you a safe homeward journey) instead of a simple goodbye.

This is in keeping with the Celtic tradition where all of life lies under God's watchful eye and He desires to meet with us in every minute of every tiny daily chore. Instead of setting aside special times of prayer and worship, all of life should be filled with these holy moments. Consequently, there were prayers and blessings for the lighting of the fire,

church.                    Port au Prince

the milking of the cows, and the making of the bed. Every opportunity was taken to use the seemingly mundane to reflect and be reminded of God's presence. Today as Irish Catholics pass a chapel they will cross themselves. Perhaps some of these rituals have become empty superstition practiced by those with a primarily cultural kind of faith, but for others it is a very real reminder of God as they journey to work or the shops.

And could it be that sometimes our most inarticulate and simple cries for help are a reaching for the transcendent, just as they are in the book of Psalms? Many of the Psalms are much more like confused cries to make some sense out of tragedy than they are stately prayers.

I remember feeling guilty for my response when, as a seventeen year old on my first trip to a large Canadian city, I found myself so overwhelmed by the skyscrapers downtown that I was left almost speechless. I was so much in awe of their immensity that all that escaped from my mouth was a cry of amazement using the Lord's name. Today I would be less likely to be so hard on myself and much freer to see myself as a ragamuffin gripped in the jaws of wonder.

When the news came across the radio on Saturday August 15, 1998 that a bomb had exploded in Omagh during the busiest part of the afternoon, many of the residents of my island let out that seemingly careless shriek of pain and

despair. The words, "Oh my God, no!" were an honest and vulnerable response to a situation where no other words could articulate our loss. Twenty-nine people died in that tragic moment. Everyone in the country seemed to know someone who was mourning a loved one or friend. All of us were ragamuffins shrieking in pain, our minds and hearts in tatters, left shaking our heads and searching our souls for meaning. Sometimes we can pray with great assurance and faith. At times like this, however, our prayers are usually ragged, and our certainties about life feel as though they are unraveling. Bruce Cockburn wrote of these as times when "the fraying rope gets closer to breaking." The prayers we pray during such moments in our life are honest and vulnerable, when we feel as though we have come to the very end of ourselves and know there is no human solution in sight. They are prayers of dependence, relying upon a grace that though asked for, still surprises us when it comes.

In the days following that great tragedy, many of us found ourselves crying out with words that some might have considered to be uncomfortably near to blasphemy—and it's admittedly a thin line—but we were heard by a God who is "the Comforter," not "the explainer." I reckon He was angry too.

My nearly inarticulate first responses to the tragedy eventually gave way to more carefully considered words. Here is the prayer I prayed on BBC Radio Ulster the following Friday:

## IN A WEEK LIKE THIS

Lord, we come to the end of another week
Except that it hasn't been just another week
It has been the worst week of our lives
And even worse for some
Lord, help us to be honest, vulnerable, and somehow hopeful in the reflection of our feelings.

Lord, we have been shocked
Shocked by how one tiny second can tear our lives apart
Shocked by how far humanity can fall
Shocked by how callous and painful our actions can be, how low we can stoop.

Lord, we are grieving
Grieving for the loss of lives with so much love and energy still to give
Grieving for the man and woman and child we will never be able to hold again
Grieving that our history is so sad and twisted.

Lord, we are confused
Confused at why this should happen
Confused about how this should happen to the innocent
Confused about where You and faith enter into these events.

Lord, we have been angry
Angry at why we allowed our family and friends to go shopping
Angry at how evil people could rip our world asunder
Angry that You allowed it to happen.

*maple , oak , elm leaves in rain*

LORD, WE ARE SEEKING
SEEKING SOME KIND OF FEEBLE CONSOLATION IN THE MIDST OF OUR DELUGE OF TEARS
SEEKING SOME KIND OF HOPE THAT GOOD MIGHT COME FROM THIS EVIL
SEEKING YOUR SPIRIT, WHOM JESUS CALLED A COMFORTER, TO WHISPER INTO OUR MADDENING SILENCE.

LORD, WE ARE SQUINTING FOR FAITH
FAITH THAT THE MAJORITY MIGHT HAVE SOME KIND OF A SAY IN THE FUTURE
FAITH THAT LOVE WILL END OUR HATE, GOOD WILL END OUR EVIL,
AND GRACE WILL TOUCH OUR BROKEN HEARTS
FAITH IN A GOD WHO IS AS ANGRY AS WE ARE
AND WHO IS REACHING OUT HIS HAND TO US.

LORD, WE ARE REMEMBERING
REMEMBERING THOSE WHO TODAY CAN NO LONGER BE SHOCKED, GRIEVE, BE ANGRY, BE CONFUSED, SEEK OR SQUINT FOR FAITH
REMEMBERING THAT YOU WATCHED AS YOUR SON, COVERED IN BLOOD, DIED AT THE FUTILE WHIM OF INJUSTICE
REMEMBERING THAT HIS DEATH IS THE ONLY THING WE CAN GROPE AFTER IN THE DARK OF A WEEK LIKE THIS.

LORD, WE HAVE PLANTED OUR LOVED ONES DEEP IN THE BLOODY EARTH OF
IRELAND THIS WEEK
WE HAVE WATERED THEM WITH OUR TEARS
LORD, MAY YOU ALLOW THEM TO BE SEEDS OF A LOVE THAT WILL GROW INTO OUR PEACE.
LORD, REMEMBER US.

AMEN.

THE THIN LINE *Steve Stockman* ✺

'garden gate'     Franklin, Tennessee    1998

DEEPER WALK *Ashley Cleveland*

*This is what I know of prayer: It is best done often and on my knees. I have found that the distracted chats with God while I'm driving do not bring the same melody that I hear in a quiet place.*

IT'S STILL DARK OUTSIDE AND I AM HALF ASLEEP
MY PRAYERS THEY SLIP AND SLIDE; I KNOW MY TALK IS CHEAP
FOR I AM EVER WANDERING, BUT I CAN HEAR YOU BECKONING

SO EVERY MORNING YOU CAN FIND ME IN THIS PLACE
AND I WILL BE WAITING; HOW I LONG TO SEE YOUR FACE
AND I WANT TO WALK THE DEEPER WALK WITH YOU

I'VE GOT THIS SILVER CHIP; NO, IT'S NOT LEGAL TENDER
AND IT'S NOT TO BARGAIN WITH; IT JUST MEANS I SURRENDER
YOU KNOW I HATE AUTHORITY, BUT I CAN'T RESIST YOUR LOVE FOR ME

SO EVERY MORNING YOU CAN FIND ME IN THIS PLACE
AND I WILL BE WAITING; HOW I LONG TO SEE YOUR FACE
AND I WANT TO WALK THE DEEPER WALK WITH YOU

SET YOUR SEAL UPON THIS REBEL GIRL
BE MY COMPANION IN THIS TEAR–STAINED WORLD

SO EVERY MORNING YOU CAN FIND ME IN THIS PLACE
AND I WILL BE WAITING; HOW I LONG TO SEE YOUR FACE
AND I WANT TO WALK THE DEEPER WALK WITH YOU

·statue of little angel·    Franklin, Tennessee 1998

## YOU WOULD'VE LIKED MY DAD.

He was a bright man, a man who reflected a spiritual radiance that matched his keen intellect. But he never drew attention to himself. He had softness about him that touched the lives of those who knew him. Lately I've met people who say things like, "Your dad was the first man who ever hugged me" or "Until I met your dad, I never knew what it meant to be a good father."

Dad helped people recognize their own value.

I'll try not to romanticize the memory of this Baptist preacher. I can remember a sermon or two where he pounded the pulpit, but more often he preached of a loving God whose sacrifice and humility had made a way for common waifs like me to cling to the robes of a King. It was this characteristic of humility which endeared him to everyone who knew him. Even those who didn't attend his church (or any for that matter) respected him. Those who didn't know him called him "Reverend." He never informed them he hated that title; he knew they meant well. But to me he'd say, "I'm no one to be revered."

Dad was so approachable that I'd sometimes confess my sins to him, probably not a norm for fathers and sons. He would listen carefully and respond empathetically, saying, "You're not the only one who has been there." He demonstrated the grace of God so consistently throughout my childhood that it was an impossible thing to refute. There was something about my parents' home that made you feel like Jesus was lounging across from you on the couch.

Perhaps that "something" was Dad.

I was so close to my father that for much of my adult life I feared the day death would take him. I couldn't imagine coping with that loss. Now it's the fact that he may live on that causes me to grieve. The man I write of in such glowing terms seems to be gone. And my wish that he have a long life seems to have been cruelly fulfilled.

Dad has Alzheimer's Disease.

At least that's what the doctors tell us, although they don't seem to be absolutely certain. Meanwhile we keep losing pieces of Dad. Or perhaps I should say that Dad keeps bequeathing bits of himself to us for safekeeping. Like the thirty-some years he spent preaching in Rhode Island, which are now ours to remember, not his. His childhood is ours as well—what exists is what we can remember of what he used to remember. It's hard enough to keep track of your own memories. No wonder people tend to become historical revisionists.

He no longer remembers growing up among the "plain people" of Lancaster County, Pennsylvania. He doesn't know that his pacifism was forged there among the Mennonites and the Amish. He doesn't know that he preached against the Vietnam War. He doesn't remember Vietnam. He doesn't know that marrying my Lutheran mother influenced the worship at the Baptist church he pastored for more than three decades. He doesn't remember that he allowed me to listen to the Beatles or that he let me get a drum set back when there was no Christian outlet for rock and roll. He doesn't remember believing that God could somehow make use of talents that didn't seem to fit into Christendom in 1966.

He doesn't know why so many people hold him so dear. He doesn't remember the weddings, baptisms, and funerals he performed for them. Or that some of them have been among his best friends for years.

We saw the Alzheimer's coming. But we kept thinking it was just old age. Even Dad would talk about it: "I've kept track of so many thousands of names over the years, that at some point my mind is going to start forgetting some of them. Don't worry."

After a long period of hopeful denial, we have come to reluctantly accept Dad's disease for what it appears to be.

Now we're reading books on the subject and my mother and my siblings and I are e-mailing each other about it. Cyber-whispering…

I've been reading up on Alzheimer's. Evidently, upsetting events in one's life can bring on the disease. I don't want to know this, as I replay the look on Dad's face the time I told him I was in a monumental crisis of faith. I told him that I felt as if I was about to step off of a cliff. Dad's disappointment and heartbreak were evident. He said, very simply, "Pray. Hope. The Lord can help you." Months down the road, I let him know that I was going to be okay. But now I own this memory that makes my eyes sad and my brow furrowed. Remembering that moment feels the way a lemon tastes.   Maybe someday I'll get a sickness that will let me forget.

I have made the transition from fearing Dad's death to fearing that he will continue living.  Early on, evidence of his memory loss wasn't so disturbing. On one visit to our home, he asked, "When did you get the dog?" I chuckled to myself. I didn't care if he remembered our dog, an animal we'd had since the previous summer. Yet when, in the same week, he didn't recognize one of my oldest and dearest friends, a person he had known for many years, I began to feel distressed. That he no longer knew this person meant that he no longer knew a part of me. Maybe that was when I first started praying, "Take him."

Most of us have a way of sorting through things to determine what to pray for. We do not do well with silence, with waiting. We ask for tangible signs of God's interest in us and cling to Scriptures that promise the things we want—prosperity, victory, and health. Some Christians even teach that you only get sick because you've sinned or you lack the faith that could heal you. I'd rather stay sick than find myself agreeing with them. I enjoyed a decade of Calvinism before Something brought me to the Canterbury Trail, to Anglicanism. Though Anglicanism has brought many changes in me, I've retained the need to explain things, to make logic out of chaos, to make good out of evil, and to see Dad's Alzheimer's as part of some Divine Plan. I make a lousy mystic.

Symbolism is not a big part of the evangelical world I grew up in and still travel in. But now I've taken to making the sign of the cross over my children as they sleep and blessing them in the name of the Father, the Son, and the Holy Spirit. I want to make the sign of the cross on my father's shining brow, but all the crossing in the world will not bring him back.

Help Thou my unbelief.

Each summer, when we visit my parents, a hometown friend throws a clambake for our family and many of our old friends from the church in Barrington. Dad enjoys the food, smiles a lot, and is the first to leave. He seems uncomfortable. Of course he does. How can he help but think to himself: Who are all these people?

After all his years of serving these very people, everything he taught them about sacrifice and humility is being lived out in them. He's still giving to them and he doesn't even know it. His illness provides the opportunity for them to live out the very things he lived out. Kindness. Caring. Compassion. Maybe that is one of the ways God is using this curse for the good. But finding a reason for living with this doesn't make me feel any better about it.

I dread calling home. I'm always hoping that Mom answers. But talking with her is not without pain—knowing that I am the first person who will actually listen to her today. It's painful to hear her tell me over the phone how many games of Skip-Bo and Rummikub she and Dad played today. I wonder if this disease will kill her before it takes him.

On Sundays during the "Prayers for the People," the Book of Common Prayer suggests a pause to allow people to add their own individual petitions. My dad's name is on the list. It is soothing to hear a stranger reading, "We pray for Phil Madeira's father." One morning a fellow parishioner named Marshall tells me, "I'd like to know more about your father." I tell him and he promises to pray for the whole family.

What we all yearn for is to be known.

It occurs to me that the sign of the cross on my children's forehead is just that. A mark that says: You are God's. You are known by Him.

Dad and Mom continue to pray together every morning and every night, as they have done throughout their fifty years of marriage. I have this to be thankful for: He knows enough to pray.

He knows he belongs to God.

I remember the last time the family was together at Dad's house in Barrington, Rhode Island. We were out on the back porch, where so many summer evenings have passed with laughter, argument, and conversation. My dad, with faltering voice and tears lining his face, offered a prayer of blessing: "Dear Lord, thank You for this wonderful family." We all contained ourselves—something we are not known for doing—glancing in wonderment at each another, choking back our own overflowing emotions.

BUT IN THAT MOMENT, WE ARE KNOWN.

HE KNOWS WE ARE HIS. ✸

LORD, MAKE ME AN INSTRUMENT OF YOUR PEACE. WHERE THERE IS HATRED, LET ME SOW LOVE. WHERE THERE IS INJURY, PARDON, WHERE THERE IS DOUBT, FAITH, WHERE THERE IS DESPAIR, HOPE, WHERE THERE IS DARKNESS, LIGHT, AND WHERE THERE IS SADNESS, JOY. O DIVINE MASTER, GRANT THAT I MAY NOT SO MUCH SEEK TO BE CONSOLED, AS TO CONSOLE; TO BE UNDERSTOOD, AS TO UNDERSTAND; TO BE LOVED, AS TO LOVE; FOR IT IS IN GIVING THAT WE RECEIVE—IT IS IN PARDONING THAT WE ARE PARDONED; AND IT IS IN DYING THAT WE ARE BORN TO ETERNAL LIFE. **ST. FRANCIS ASSISI** ✸

In 1982 I was traveling home to Kansas City with my wife Bernadette and our two-year-old daughter Alicia after a trip to California. We were enjoying our flight when Alicia began to experience difficulty in breathing. We were puzzled at first, but the situation seemed to grow worse and we began to grow alarmed. Alicia got to the point where she could barely catch her breath and was gasping so badly that the flight attendant had to provide her with oxygen.

After we landed at home, her breathing got even worse. When we called the doctor, he told us to take her straight to the hospital, where she was put in the children's ward. Her little eyes were filled with tears from the strain of coughing and the difficulty of breathing. The doctors were finally able to diagnose her condition as "croup," and they placed her in an oxygen tent overnight. She looked so small, so fragile, and so vulnerable in that big oxygen tent. It nearly broke our hearts.

Bernadette and I had lost a little baby before, so our hearts were heavy and filled with concern. We began to pray for Alicia. We prayed intensely. By the next day, she looked a little better and her breathing had improved. Bernadette and I sat on the edge of the bed and held her tiny hand. We smiled at her and she smiled back.

Our gentle moment was interrupted by a sound from the adjoining room—a deep and terrible gasping cough, similar to what Alicia was beginning to recover from. The child next door was probably suffering from the same affliction. Bernadette and I looked at each other, silently communicating our sympathy for the parents who were facing turmoil similar to ours. Then Alicia, only two years old, firmly spoke these words: "We need to pray for that child!" At her tender young age, Alicia was just beginning to talk, so her words came as a surprise. But she knew in her heart what needed to be done. We needed to pray. So we did. The three of us together.

Alicia recognized the need of that hurting, coughing child and felt a sort of solidarity with her. She did not need a suggestion from us, her parents. In her young heart she knew instinctively what needed to be done. In the midst of her own struggle with illness she seemed to forget about herself and focus on the need of another, and to know that the best way to help was to lift that other child up into the hands of our loving Heavenly Father.

I could not help but think of the words of Jesus: "EXCEPT YOU BECOME AS A LITTLE CHILD..." Alicia, who soon recovered, had provided for us a beautiful example of what prayer is meant to be. ✸

PRAYER OF A NOWHERE MAN *Kevin Max*

I'M A REAL NOWHERE MAN,
SITTING IN THIS "NOWHERE LAND"
WITH JUST TOO MANY PLACES TO GO.
A CRUSTY BIT OF ADAM'S HEART,
A DIRTY PUDDLE OF HIS ART,
A MIRACLE OF BROKEN STRINGS.

WITH THESE THINGS,
I SING AND DANCE
AND FULFILL MY INHERITANCE.
I DIDN'T HAVE A POINT OF VIEW,
UNTIL THE SKIES WERE FILLED WITH YOU,
SO PERFECT AND SO RELEVANT
YOUR EYES LOOK DOWN ON ME.

I'M A BIT LIKE ALL OF US,
HOUSED IN GREY MATTER
WITH VIBRANT YELLOWS.
A TRANSPARENT WANDERING THING
WITH A WILL BIGGER THAN THE SEA.
AREN'T I A BIT LIKE YOU AND ME?
FILLED WITH ALL THE MYSTERY
OF ONE THAT WILL COME AGAIN,
AND SET FREE ALL THE BEARS,
WITH RAGAMUFFIN HAIR.

BROKEN *Ben Pearson*

Broken...I now talk with God.

O Lord Jesus my savior.

Today my heart is empty.

Pride is the thing I will miss least when time comes to an end.

I need a priest.

I need a preacher.

I need an exorcist to banish the snake I've been handling called...self.

I need You.

Broken...I now talk to God.

*"I have had prayers answered—most strangely so sometimes—but I think our heavenly Father's loving-kindness has been even more evident in what He has refused me."* —*Lewis Carroll, from* The Letters of Lewis Carroll

The first time I pray to God—I mean actually and earnestly talk to the air in the hope someone is really there—is during a Boy Scout camping trip. After a five-mile hike there isn't enough room to fit everyone in the truck sent to retrieve us, so I am left all alone on the prairie to wait for one of the adults to come back. Because of some mixed signals he doesn't, at least not for over six or seven hours, after sunset, and after the point where I believe I will die from exposure, starvation, coyotes, or rattlesnakes. It is more like a pity party than a prayer. *Why me? I'm too young to die. It'll serve them right for leaving me. God, if You can hear me, help me. Help someone find me.* Someone does. Finally.

I suppose God heard me. I can't say whether He answered my prayer or whether someone finally realized I was long overdue. Maybe God reminded them. Maybe He kept the coyotes and rattlesnakes away. Or maybe I was too skinny and full of self-pity for their taste.

A few years later…My family begins to attend a church. One Sunday evening at a youth meeting, the leader, Ron, asks me to say an opening prayer. I have never prayed aloud in front of people. I try to sound religious and sincere, fumbling along, borrowing phrases from adult prayers. *Dear God, thank You for this day and…uh, this place and…uh, this opportunity to meet and…uh, be with us, and…uh,* (long pause) *in Jesus' name. Amen.* (I sound like Mr. Stamps, my seventh-grade Texas history teacher. He is so boring we pass the time counting how many times he says, "and…uh" during the class. His record was fifty-seven).

I remember feeling embarrassed, inept, exposed as an amateur prayer. Ron's prayers were relaxed and real talk. He spoke to God reverently but naturally, in his everyday tone, not in a from-the-pulpit style. I don't know how God felt about my prayer. Maybe He yawned and counted the "and...uhs." Maybe He was just glad to hear from me at all.

Two years later...early June...Thursday night, during a "night of silence" at church camp, I sit on a picnic table under a clear, star-filled sky talking to God. I have not yet seen great evil or suffering, death or despair close up. (My worst sins involve lying and stealing Coke bottles from open garages.) Over the last year, I have been coming to some sense of my fragile and obscure position in the universe. Any feeling of need for God is recent, mainly because I lost my virginity this spring and for the first time I feel like a sinner, like I have deliberately gone against God's will in a big way. So in simple language, without understanding how it all works, I tell God I believe and ask Him to forgive me and save me through the sacrifice Jesus made and to take me to heaven some day when I die. I cannot describe the overwhelming sense of comfort and the lift in my heart that occurs in the next moments. Through the tears and silence a lightness, a tender nearness, and a loving embrace come over me like I have never known. I am consoled and know I am forgiven, accepted, and out from under any condemnation from God. I experience a calm euphoria.

Even now, as I describe that experience, my heart softens and reconnects with a reality no philosopher or psychologist can explain away.

Three years later...One month before graduation, the high school guidance counselor calls me to her office. With great pleasure she informs me I have been granted a full four-year scholarship to any university of my choosing in the state of Texas because of my scoliosis—curvature of the spine—a condition my dad discovered a year earlier when he saw me doing a few shirtless push-ups to enhance my hundred and ten pound physique. She explains that a surplus of Texas oil revenue has been set aside to ensure productive lives for physically challenged citizens. Without my knowledge she applied for me.

Many of my buddies know by February of our senior year where they will attend college in the fall. I have done more praying about the future than sending out applications, more out of fuzzy-headed procrastination than any deep spiritual reliance on the hand of Providence.

A year later… I lie in a hospital bed in Houston the night before surgery. For two years I have prayed to be healed from scoliosis. I remember the place in the Bible where Jesus said, "Whatever you ask of the Father in my name, He will give you." I use his own words like a contractual clause He must live up to. Like a checkmate move on the Almighty. *Dear God, please heal me before morning, in Jesus' name.* Before daylight the nurses come in, wheel me off to the O.R., where a team of specialists cut my back open like a watermelon, fuse seven vertebrae, screw two steel rods into my bones and stitch me up. I spend the next nine months in a body cast. During the incubation of that unanswered prayer, I learn to play the guitar, scour the New Testament beginning to end, and become good friends with my mother, Oteka, who takes such good care of me.

I see now what Lewis Carroll meant. God refused me this request and answered strangely. That year was a critical turning point of my life. Being marooned (although more briefly than Robinson Crusoe) redirected my life. I had other (and perhaps more serious) ailments to be delivered from than scoliosis, and other prayers that took priority on the Great Physician's chart. Lack of faith. Focus. Life direction. Discipline. I read the Bible daily and practiced the guitar for hours on end. I discovered a personal faith that replaced the one gathered secondhand, and tapped into an undeveloped musical gift that would become my vocation. Where would I be today if God had healed my back that night?

Spring of 1979…En route to Fort Worth, Texas from Austin I write a lullaby called "Dream A Dream." It is a song to sing a child to sleep. Before I know it I am crying as I drive down the Interstate. A deep longing has surfaced. I imagine singing it to my own daughter one day and pray, *Dear God, give me a little girl to sing this to someday.*

Nineteen springs later, Emmaline Willow Grace is born—the right audience and the answer to my prayer.

February 1980…About 2:00 A.M. I wake up with a tickle deep in the back of my throat. Instantly I know it's that cough coming back, the same cough I have had on and off every winter since I caught severe bronchitis in Iceland in 1975. It always starts this way. The tickle. Then the catch when I take a deep breath, followed by congestion which turns into a full-blown, sleep-depriving hack that lasts for weeks. This time I have had it. I am angry. Sitting up in bed in the dark I ask God in irritated tones to PLEASE heal this cough. *I know You can. You can do anything. So will You PLEASE? In Jesus' name.* I go back to sleep.

The next afternoon I realize the tickle is not there anymore. It will be back that night I figure. But the next day, there is no tickle. It takes me three days to consider myself healed. Even longer to believe it. The tickle is not there. And the chronic "walking bronchitis," as one doctor called it, never returns. Answered prayer? Or a virus unable to thrive in angry host?

The next year…I fall in love with a young woman I want—more than anything—to spend my life with. She falls in love with me. And out of love. And back in love with her last boyfriend. I pray every night and day for a year that her heart will turn again to me. It doesn't. They marry the next year.

Request denied.

Fall 1983…I sit in church for a Wednesday evening service. The pastor invites anyone with a need for physical healing to the front. A three-year old shoulder pain is plaguing me again. I have self-diagnosed it as a pinched nerve or muscle damage, originally injured hanging sheetrock overhead in the spring of 1980. Any fatigue or overuse of that muscle between my right shoulder and neck makes it burn and seize up. I walk to the front, and someone I don't know lays a hand on my shoulder and prays. I thank them and return to my seat.

This time it takes me several months to realize the problem is gone. To this day it has never hurt me again.

Spring 1987…My dear friend, Anita, comes down with cancer. Breast cancer. I pray. Hundreds pray. *Dear God, heal her. Give her strength to endure till healing comes. Give the doctors wisdom. Thy will be done. In Jesus' name.* The more we pray the worse the prognosis. Mastectomy. Chemotherapy. Anita loses her hair.

Anita survived that terrible year. After the thunder of that storm, there's still a light in her eyes. And she shines it on everyone, especially her grandchildren.

April 12, 1988…Climbing the stairs at my home, I collapse in tears. I am terribly lonely. For someone to share my life with. I have so many friends. But no "someone." I scribble down a prayer.:

*I am terribly lonely. For someone to share my life with.*
*I have so many friends. But no "someone." I scribble down a prayer.*

HOW MANY NIGHTS
MUST I CLIMB THE STAIRS ALONE—
DRAGGING MY HEART UP
LIKE A STONE—
SPILLING TEARS
INTO MY HANDS—
BEGGING THE SAME
OLD LINE AGAIN?

HOW MANY PIECES
MUST BE CHIPPED AWAY—
UNTIL THERE IS NOTHING
LEFT TO BREAK—
BUT ONLY AN OPEN
WOUND THAT BLEEDS—
MAKING ME FREE
AT LAST TO NEED?

WHERE IS THE TOUCH
THAT WILL RANSOM THE YEARS—
STRIP MY SOUL
OF ITS THIN VENEER—
EXPOSE MY NAKED
CRINGING MIND—
AND EMBRACE MY BODY
LIKE A CLINGING VINE?

PLEASE
HOW MANY
PLEASE
HOW MANY MORE?
PLEASE
TELL ME
PLEASE...PLEASE...PLEASE

ANNE FRANK SAID IT WELL: "A PERSON CAN BE LONELY EVEN IF HE IS LOVED BY MANY PEOPLE, BECAUSE HE IS STILL NOT THE 'ONE AND ONLY' TO ANYONE." MY ONE AND ONLY IS STILL SOME YEARS DOWN THE ROAD. AND SHE IS NOT WHO I THINK.

Saturday, November 18, 1989…In one week the woman I intend to marry and I will make our engagement official at her home. We will be married next spring. Today she stands beside her car about to drive several hours to surprise me. An older woman standing with her says a quick prayer for "traveling mercies." Nine miles down the road RosaLynn is killed in a head-on collision. I am marooned. Again. This time on an island of grief.

For the next year my main prayers are: *Dear God, keep me going* and *protect me from evil*. By which I mean extreme, unhealthy behavior—in the short term—sleepless exhaustion, drinking, even suicide. And in the long term—bitterness, cynicism, unbelief. I survive. With a little help from my friends. With a lot of help from my friends. And no doubt, their prayers. I survive that year, but do not thrive. For nine months I take up smoking, initially to keep me awake on long drives. I see too many sunrises, flicking cigarette butts into the backyard and wondering if thriving is possible.

July 1992, Barcelona, Spain…I am a guest artist at an outreach during the Olympics. One of the speakers delivers a talk asking the question: What do we do with our personal pain, which we all have, in regard to our mission in life? Do we get well and then get on with our calling? Or do we respond to our calling and get well along the way? His counsel is the second—get well along the way. We are all wounded. If we wait until we are well to be fit for our mission, life will be over. He concludes by asking us to turn to two others near us and ask for prayer for a very specific pain in our life. I turn to my Dutch friend Tjiebbo who knows me from two previous trips together in Sweden. I tell him I am coming back to life, functional and even thriving, able to enjoy so much and be useful and productive. But I still carry a fisted knot in my soul about RosaLynn's death. No doubt it is part anger, bitterness, and confusion with a sense of betrayal or unrightness about it. And I don't know how to untie it. He prays one sentence. *"Dear Lord, don't let Billy's memories remain*

*anchors that he has to drag along. Turn them to treasures he can carry with him."* I begin to feel the warm tears gather in my eyes and then drip onto my folded hands. I weep gently. No tumult. No great upheaval.

That's all Tjiebbo prays. We sit in silence for a minute or so. Then he counsels me to re-check and let go of any unspoken "vows" I may have made like "remaining single" or "finding a manageable level of melancholy," instead of coming fully back to the land of the living. (Thoreau called it "quiet desperation.")

In less than fifteen minutes I am different. Lighter. The knot in my soul is gone. I take a deeper breath than I have taken in over two years.

The most surprising thing of all is what replaces the knot. Gratitude. I am actually grateful. For RosaLynn. For knowing her. For the time we had. I am thankful for the tenacious love of so many along the way. And thankful to God, Who in those moments answered so many prayers.

Saturday October 22, 1994…I am standing at the front of a church. Next to me is my "One and Only," Kellie. We are dressed in our finest. Most of my "please" prayer of April 12, 1988 is about to be answered. The pastor declares us husband and wife, then prays to God to bless our marriage and the children we will have.

I don't know how much or which prayers influence or change God's mind. I am aware that the Bible says, "The Lord is near. Do not be anxious about anything, but in everything, by prayer and petition, present your requests to God. And the peace of God, which transcends all understanding, will guard hearts and minds in Christ Jesus" (Philippians 4:5-7 NIV). Perhaps, as C.S. Lewis maintained, prayer may have more to do with influencing me than God anyway.

I still pray for traveling mercies when a friend leaves on a trip. I pray for troubled marriages to be mended. Some of them are, and some end in divorce. In that event we pray for their kids or, *Dear God, don't let their wounds be anchors they have to drag along. Turn them to teachers and treasures they can carry with them.*

We pray over meals. At bedtime. *Dear God, watch over our Willow and Wyatt in the night. By your angels keep them safe 'til morning light and make their spirits soft and bright. In Jesus name, Amen.* More and more I pray part or all of what Jesus prayed. Our Father in heaven…

Prayer is a bulletin board where I post memos to the Almighty. It is not a chess game where I negotiate to get God to see or do things my way. He knows how it looks through my eyes. He knows how to manage a universe. Prayer isn't a way to see things like He does. It's a refuge. An oasis of spiritual life. When I don't go there, I dry up. And brown. Like my yard.

I don't go very long without water. Sometimes, though, I neglect or avoid prayer deliberately, like ignoring my wife or a friend because of an issue I don't want to face. But the restless, unnatural isolation of life as a lone ranger draws me back like a thirst. A thirst for intimacy, I suppose. For nearness, acceptance, consolation. Sometimes in prayer, the lightness and calm euphoria return.

The longer I live the shorter my prayers become. At least the spoken part. Sometimes it's just stargazing and saying, "Thanks for the evening, it was heavenly." Prayer becomes listening more than petitioning. It is like sitting by a stream. Watching the movement. Unable to read the hieroglyphic of light on the surface, but consoled by it nonetheless. "I pour my heart out like water," the prophet Jeremiah said. Sometimes in tears. Sometimes in anger or confusion. Often in gratitude. Often in silence. Always in longing. I WAIT. THE RIVER BENDS TOWARD ME. OR I AM MOVED TOWARD IT—TOWARD THE PRESENCE OF GOD. WHENEVER THIS HAPPENS THE CURRENT CARRIES ME. TO DEEP, STILL WATER. AND I GREEN. ✸

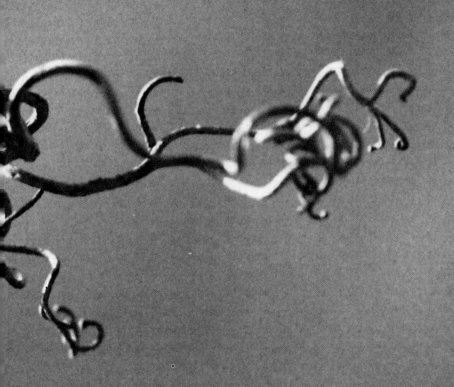

GOD GRANT ME TEARS *Rick Elias*

For me, learning to pray has been a journey, a journey that parallels my relationship with God. Slowly and over time, I have come to understand a little more about what it means to pour out my soul to God in my prayer. Through all the twists and turns of that journey, I've learned that the deepest prayers are those that arise from the pain and brokenness in our lives.

Because I grew up in a Catholic home, I knew the Lord's Prayer (which I'd learned in Catechism class) and other liturgical prayers from an early age. I guess they didn't mean much to me as a child. I didn't really understand them very well. They were just words. I had the sense that these were prayers that had existed for thousands of years, but I didn't see them as relevant to me. God didn't seem very approachable, so I didn't see prayer as much more than a good ritual to perform. I didn't have a clear sense that I was actually praying to someone.

When I was 16, I went on a Youth for Christ outreach. By this time my mother had been divorced and excommunicated, so we had not gone to any church for a long time. In fact, my home was pretty heavily steeped in

belief in reincarnation, spirits, and astrology. And I was a very troubled young man. I went on an outreach and felt completely befuddled by the young evangelical Christians who seemed perfectly comfortable with the notion that we could talk directly with God, without the intervention of a priest. This was a new concept to me, but I embraced it whole-heartedly. I wanted to be able to talk with God.

Over the next several years I became pretty serious about my faith. I sought a personal relationship with God so earnestly that I was a lot more zealous about it than most of my friends. Their main reason for involvement in Youth for Christ was that it was an opportunity to get together socially and have a good time. But I wanted to know God more intimately. I started to look for a church to attend. Now this was about the time of the Jesus movement, so I bounced around a little, and got involved in some pretty freaky churches, many of them weird hippie churches. Through their influence, I was indoctrinated into some very legalistic and off-the-wall teaching.

When it was time to decide on college, I chose a Christian school. This turned out to be a tragic mistake. Most of the kids who attended were preacher's kids, and I found myself an outcast. There were two dorms at the school—one right on campus, and one on the hill where all the outcasts lived. I, of course, ended upon the hill! I never fit into the system and began to struggle with all kinds of questions. What I didn't get were meaningful answers. This led to a complete meltdown in my faith. I felt like I was in a Cessna that flew straight into a cliff. Boom! I collided with an immovable object. I wound up leaving the college or being thrown out, depending upon who you talk to. And I turned my back on Christianity. Most people remember the day they were saved. But I remember the day I renounced my faith, saying, "Forget this. It's stupid. If this is what Christianity is, I want no part of it."

Ironically, I made my renunciation as a prayer to God. It wasn't so much Jesus with whom I was fed up, but Christianity as I had come to know it. So I spent the next ten years running away from faith. They were years of bad choices, of being self-destructive. But there was good that came out of these years. The process was a lot like tearing down a house. You soon find out what's in the walls and how the plumbing works. Well, I found out a lot about myself through trying to destroy myself. I discovered who I really was, and I uncovered a lot about myself that I didn't like. THROUGH THAT WHOLE PROCESS, I REMEMBER HEARING GOD CALL LOUDER AND LOUDER,

MAKING HIMSELF MORE AND MORE EVIDENT THROUGH LITTLE THINGS IN MY LIFE. I WASN'T LOOKING FOR JESUS CHRIST, BUT HE WAS LOOKING FOR ME. AND THEN CAME A MOMENT WHICH I CAN ONLY DESCRIBE AS MIRACULOUS, one of the few times I can say that I really felt God invade my consciousness and speak to my heart. God's message to me was similar to the one I would later hear Rich Mullins give night after night when I toured with him: There is nothing I can do to make God love me more and there is nothing I can do to make Him love me less. Newly embracing God's love, I began once again to pursue a relationship with Christ.

Life is a process. I'm not always happy with who I am—I can certainly use a lot of work—but I've come to accept the fact that God does love me. The acceptance of His love is my foundation. Everything else is secondary. I'll always have stuff to work on in my life (which I may or may not succeed at changing), but I know God loves me as I am. I've accepted the fact that I'm a broken person. Just flat-out broken.

At the end of the video documentary on Rich Mullins, Brennan Manning quotes a line from a well-known play: "In love's service, only wounded soldiers exist." That line is so absolutely true. You must be broken to be used by God. When you're broken, you know you need something more in your life. Once you've done all you can do and tried hard to fix everything you don't like about yourself, you might even convince yourself that you've done a pretty good job of it. But you'd be fooling yourself. At the end of the day, you really are completely and utterly dependent upon God's mercy and grace to cover what will never be completely fixed in you.

Recognizing your brokenness is absolutely the only way you can approach God. All of us are broken in one way or another. No one can approach God with confidence in their own personal holiness. Instead, we must admit our failings and inadequacies. It's not important to worry about being presentable. The important thing is to come to Him in humility. The title of an old Welsh prayer called "God Grant Me Tears," really captures the essence of how we should pray. As we admit our brokenness, God gives us a new sense of purpose and meaning. We understand our place on this planet. We see that His love is our only real hope. ✸

I guess I should start out by saying I'm not even sure what *la vida loca* means, but I suspect it is a huge national threat…to men in particular. Have you seen that guy? How can mere mortals compete with that? My fiancée says he's no big deal, but I bet if she had to take a polygraph while looking at a Ricky Martin video…well, I'm sure I wouldn't want to know the results.

To make matters worse, he's just informed us that to be a happy, complete person we have to make sure we're livin' *la vida loca*. Again, I don't really know what that means, but judging by appearance, appearance is everything. We need to have lots of money, a different date every night, perfect teeth, abs of steel, nerves of steel… and we must never lose our will to boogie. Just thinking about it makes me want a really long nap in the worst way. So I've been praying for this new lifestyle, but it is kinda hard to ask for. How does one attain la vida loca? I've been asking, but God has been unusually quiet on the subject. One could begin to suspect that maybe these things aren't so important as MTV or VH1 would have us believe. But would VH1 lie to us?

Maybe it's not that difficult to question the latest music videos, but they are not alone in propagating this message. It seems that a lot of the televangelists are preaching a very similar gospel. If we are in God's will, they assure us, we will be wealthy, healthy, prosperous, God-fearing white upper-middle class Republicans. Could they be lying to us?

An interesting observation strikes me. It seems that most of our prayers, goals, and conversations revolve around what we need to obtain in order to be happy. We ask God to give us happiness, peace, money, girlfriends or boyfriends, and husbands or wives—all of which are okay things to want (unless you're praying for a girlfriend or boyfriend when you already have a husband or wife.) But the underlying assumption is that we have to "get" something to be more fulfilled. We rarely speak of the peace that comes from giving things up, going without, asking God to take something from us—even if it's something we think we want. Instead of spending our prayer time asking God for His will in our lives, we end up telling Him what we think His will ought to be. Why is it so hard to remember that so many good things come to our lives through trials, pain, and general doing-without or taking-away?

There is a certain wing of the evangelical church that believes that if we say the right thing the right way, pray with just the right words, and present ourselves in the right manner as virtuous, godly folk—God is obligated to do what we ask of Him. At that point He becomes our servant. This strikes me as a form of witchcraft, an attempt to trick God into making us healthy, wealthy, and happy. This doesn't seem to reconcile very well with the message of Job!

There is a tendency among some of us Christians to reduce prayer to a kind of magic formula that gets us what we want or think we need. Or maybe we think that it gives us a special "inside track" into the mind of God. We've developed a pretty weird view of how God communicates with us. Sometimes we act as if we believe God is feeding us information on a moment—by—moment basis. Though I do believe that God does some pretty amazing, supernatural things to get our attention, we should not labor under the notion that God is going to show up and tell us what kind of groceries to buy or what kind of strings we should put on our guitar. We open ourselves to all kinds of dangers when we have this expectation. It's all too easy to mistake our emotions for God's voice, and as mistakes go, that's a pretty big one.

So what is prayer? When we pray, we are speaking aloud to someone we cannot prove exists. We launch our prayers heavenward in the belief that they break through the boundaries of our own minds and lives. I tried to capture this truth in a recent song I wrote called "Bouncing Off the Ceiling": SOMETIMES I GET THE FEELING MY PRAYERS BOUNCE RIGHT OFF THE CEILING, AND THEY SPIN AROUND THE ROOM WITH ME AND NEVER GET TO GET TO YOU. AND THOUGH MY HEAD IS REELING, I WILL STILL GO ON BELIEVING THAT THEY'LL FLY LIKE HOLY MISSILES, AND TEAR A HOLE RIGHT THROUGH THE ROOF.

We pray with the confidence that God is real, that there is Someone who hears us and cares for us. Maybe this *la vida loca* stuff is over—rated. Maybe when we seem to get less it's because God really wants more for us. Maybe He really does love us so much that He will take away anything that would affect our relationship with Him. Maybe the Bible is true and VH1 (and some of those preachers) are a little misguided. Thinking about my spiritual *la vida loca* (my crazy spiritual life) helps me realize afresh how much I am loved in the midst of everything. Maybe that's what really matters most after all. ✸

"Here we are again, Lord, over and over, again and one more time we come before You."

When I heard these words of prayer, they grabbed my attention. They came from one of the elders of a little Baptist church where I was filling in as a drummer. The choir's regular drummer was ill, so I'd been called at the last minute and asked to help out with the music for this meeting. The speaker that afternoon was a passionate preacher whose call and response, half singing-half talking style challenged the congregation to a deeper commitment of faith. Once he finished, the speaker sat down and the pastor stood to his feet, calling on one of the elders to pray.

The man who got to his feet was wearing an old light blue suit and dark glasses. He must have been in his eighties, and it was obvious that he was nearly blind. He rocked back and forth for just a moment, obviously composing himself, then cleared his throat and spoke these words: "Here we are again, Lord, over and over, again and one more time we come before You."

He repeated the phrase as he spoke to God from his heart. "Here we come, over and over, again and one more time. We have sinned and we can't make it on our own. We're weak. Here we are again." The words struck me so powerfully that I pulled a pencil from my pocket and wrote the phrase down: *Over and over, again and one more time*. I thought of all the experiences in the life of this elderly gentleman, about all that he had been through in his long life. And through it all he had learned a powerful lesson about the nature of God.

WE MAY FAIL OVER AND OVER. WE MAY KEEP TRYING AND KEEP FAILING. BUT GOD IS ALWAYS THERE. HE IS ALWAYS FAITHFUL. ALWAYS FORGIVING. HE'S BIG ENOUGH TO DEAL WITH THE BIGGEST CHALLENGES IN OUR LIVES. WE CAN TRUST HIM. Learning to trust begins with prayer. Prayer is the place where we can totally expose ourselves to God. We can be honest. We do not have to be afraid of coming clean about all the junk that arises in the course of living out our lives. In prayer we can struggle with all the difficult things life throws at us, ask the troubling questions that don't seem to have any easy answers, and struggle with God, just as Jacob did.

We don't have to be afraid to tell God exactly what is on our mind. We don't have to learn any special lingo or pray in some particular way or by a specific set of rules. I've learned that I can go to God and tell Him everything, tell Him the things I can't tell anyone else. After all, He already knows everything about me. It would be foolish to think I can hide anything from Him. Instead, I need to confess it and get on with it. I can come clean with God because He hears me and really loves me. And He forgives me.

If we learn to be honest before God, it also helps us learn to be honest with other people. Rich Mullins was like that—honest before God and other with others. I got to know him somewhat as a member of the Ragamuffin Band. He never worried about putting up a façade or pretending to be someone special. Rich was himself, with all his faults and failings. No frills. I personally have known very few people who walk the walk and talk the talk. Rich Mullins was one of them. I learned from him that we can touch the lives of others most powerfully when we come as we are, open about our failings and shortcomings, not pretending to be spiritual superstars.

There is a freedom in being honest with God that surpasses the honesty we can have with even our closest friends. When I pray honestly to God, it reminds me how much I need His grace and mercy. If I want to remain in His will and see my life continue to change, I have to make it a priority to spend time with Him. I don't know how I'd be able to function without this kind of intimate relationship with Him. Life is extremely challenging. So many things can distract and corrupt. Being honest with God helps me shed my carefully constructed façade. It eases my burdens and helps me approach my life realistically and hopefully.

Therefore, I try to discipline myself to pray and read the Word of God at the beginning of every day, though I am not always successful. Time spent with God strengthens my spirit, puts me in His protective armor, and lets me "lay my burdens down." It gives me a clearer vision of God's will for my life and whets my appetite to spend more time with Him. And when I pray, I better understand who I am. I realize I'm not in control and that there is Someone greater than me to whom I must present my life. I am humbled. Prayer wakes me up to the bigger world around me and reminds me that there is One who loves me and will walk with me even through my failings. He is always there.

WE CAN COME AS WE ARE. OVER AND OVER...AGAIN AND ONE MORE TIME. ✸

there's a little book that my friend kristen made for me. it's small and blue and perfect for hiding in when i am afraid or secretly happy. though i can't exactly crawl inside of it, i do try to write myself onto the clean white pages. it is my book of common prayer, a liturgy of my heart journaled over the last three years. most of the prayers are along the lines of "dear God, hi. i am crazy. send help soon."

but once in a while thanksgiving is celebrated and it's more along the lines of "hello darling Father, you're monstrously kind and i am completely taken with your very tender care for me." whatever the tone, i take a great deal of comfort in believing that these small, often desperate words are somehow being magically transformed into something acceptable in the sight of my Creator.

His kingdom has come. and with it, an invitation to become "the righteousness of God…His sons and daughters." i am learning to live within the salvation and confrontation of "Thy kingdom come" and "Thy will be done." even in the midst of all my fears, i am growing in relationship with my Father. i am learning how to pray.

the prayers that I have scribbled in my blue book are not sophisticated…but i think they are heard. i want to believe i have the freedom to speak out my hopes to God, even when i don't have the words…i want to believe He understands my dumbfounded cries, the "goo-goo ga-ga" that arises in response to life's severe unpredictability. what all my baby—like chatter really means is, "come Lord Jesus."

it's a very great vision—to become the righteousness of God, His sons and daughters, His adopted wrecks of hope—and it's only a little book with little words, but i believe they are being made new, sparkling with the shimmer of the new covenant. this is my prayer.

THE DAYLIGHT IS ITS OWN HALLELUJAH
I GUESS IT IS HELPING US TO STAND
BRINGING A HOPE LIKE THE MORNING
AND SOME THINGS I JUST DON'T UNDERSTAND

HOLY HOLY
THE BONE AND THE GOSPEL
THE WORD MADE FLESH
DWELLING AMONG US
AMONG US

THANK YOU FATHER
FOR JOY DESPITE OURSELVES
FOR NEVER REALLY BEING ALONE
THANK YOU FOR MERCY, FOR MERCY
FOR WATER THAT TASTES LIKE PEOPLE SOMETIMES
BEAUTIFUL MESSY PEOPLE
DRINKING UP THE WATER OF LIFE

YOU ARE CONSTANCY
NOT WITHHOLDING, NEVER WITHDRAWING
HELP US REMEMBER
THAT THE WORK OF LOVING YOU AND OUR NEIGHBORS
IS A JOY, A THANKSGIVING, A GIFT
AN ACT OF GRATITUDE

THANK YOU
BREAK US AND CALL US YOUR OWN
AMEN.

THIS IS MY PRAYER.

In March of 1982 I took a single gig as a sub, playing piano for a jazz saxophonist named Michael Butera. Mike was a Christian of the born-again variety. I was determined not to hold it against him! I had been praying to the God of the Bible for twelve months or so, asking for only a couple things really: sobriety and work. Both were coming slowly, little by little, like the drip of a faucet. Perhaps the God of the Christians was alive and well, listening to the pleas of the foolish after all. At the end of the long night of making music, I thanked Mike for hiring me and let him know that I was grateful for the work.

A month later I received a phone call from Mike. I expected that he might have another gig for me, but instead he hesitated just a moment before getting to the point of his call. It seems that God had strongly impressed upon Mike that he should contact me and ask if we could meet together and pray. I could tell that he was trying to be very sensitive and respectful toward me and careful not to come across as weird. It seemed like an odd request, but I tried my best to put him at ease.

"I pray all the time," I told him. "Come on over."

Mike wasted no time. He was at my door within minutes and I ushered him in. As it turned out, he'd really come to tell me the story of Jesus. Since then I've learned that to tell someone the story of Jesus, to ask them to consider its truthfulness, is to say to them, "Picture this." And when truth interacts with an imagination supernaturally charged by faith—belief will announce itself. It always does.

With my imagination alive to truth and my need clear to me, I knew Mike was right: Jesus was my Savior. Time seemed to unwind and come to a stop as I imagined a line separating two lives—the life I'd been living and the one that Jesus beckoned me toward. Amazed and afraid, I knew that if I stepped over the line into life with Jesus, there would be no turning back. I WOULD HAVE TO LEAVE MY OLD LIFE BEHIND. BUT WHAT CHOICE DID I REALLY HAVE? If I refused to cross over I would be knowingly choosing to live an untruthful life. By seeing the truth but refusing to accept it, I would be the most miserable person in the world. Time came alive once again as I spoke out loud a life—defining prayer, confessing my need and requesting the kindness of God. Truth became my tears, and like the praying multitude before me, I believed.

What was begun that night in prayer has fueled my days and nights. Talking with God is one of the essentials of my existence, like blood and breath and water. It is a fountain of creativity. It is the Big Conversation that defines who I am. It's the place where I can say "thank You" and "I love You," where I can let my prayers morph from address into praise, then crossfade again into request. Prayer is filled with life and is as real and visceral and messy as life itself.

Praying is like putting on clothes in the morning. It covers my nakedness and answers the Edenic question, "Where are you, Chuck?" Through my prayers I announce my location and my status, dissolving any pretense that I am anything other than a small and needy man.

Prayers are like sirens announcing the presence and power of God. When we call, He answers. Here He comes, the prayer signals. Look out! Then the world is not the same as it was a nanosecond before. When God's will is done on earth as it is in heaven, the blind see, the lame walk, and the captives are set free. The cancer inside a young mother will disappear, a defective engine will start, a marriage will be healed, an orphan will know a parent's love, a child will cease flirting with drugs, and an angel will come to the aid of some needy human here on planet Earth. And on some days, when it's really necessary, God will send a saxophonist, carrying the words of life, riffing on a Love Supreme. ✹

PRAYERS OF A QUIET MAN  *Beaker*

I never met the man. He is little more than an old photograph, faded black and aged white; with receding hair, hardened arteries, and a pressed suit, he's frozen there, statue-like, granite and gray next to his wife, his brother's widow. That photograph holds seventy or more years—a lifetime—defining a life I do not otherwise know but for a few stories. Kentucky born and forged by a war, a depression, and a migration north to the banks of the Licking River, he found religion—or it found him.

Maybe he'd been looking for it, looking for something or someone, or maybe he had been caught completely off guard. Maybe he'd been listening. They say his words were few. Maybe he'd been listening for a song, or a voice, some sort of sound that awakened within him the soul that slept. Maybe he'd listened beyond, past, and through religion, listening for that wholly beautiful and fragile song of the invisible singer, that voice unlike any other that would someday become familiar, that sound of heaven falling and filling a heart. Behind the spectacled eyes, beneath the wrinkled skin, there lurked a quiet, listening man.

Fourteen grandchildren called him "Papaw." His five daughters and only son called him "Daddy" til the day he died in 1963. I never called him anything—born a year later to his youngest child, I am his last grandchild and her last son.

PRAYE TO
SAINT OSEPH
God Who IN Thin INEFFable
Provid nce DIDST uchsaFE T
Choose lessed Jos ph To be Th
HUSBand F Thy MOST HOLY MOTHE
Grant, w Beseech The , That We M
be Made Worthy To ave HIM For ur
INTERC SSOR IN H AVEN,
Whom EARTH We nerate AS ur
HOLY PR TECTor.
To You ho LIVEST nd REigne
Foreve and ever
AMEN

They say he prayed often, though no one ever heard him. Perhaps he found himself tied in the tongue of angel, or maybe his lips had been touched by Isaiah's burning coal—whatever the reason, he kept his prayers, his praying, a secret.

His refusal to pray aloud or in public carried even to the large gatherings around the dinner table, where before each massive meal, his wife would bless the food as he sat at the end of the table in silence—or perhaps it was not silence at all. His heart and soul and mind could speak without words. He had learned that the vocalization of his prayer wasn't necessary to gain God's attention—he had taken Christ at His word when He said, "When you pray, go into your room, close the door and pray to your Father who is unseen." But I hear his prayers sometimes—I pray them too.

I hear him in a bloody bunker—nineteen years old, a doughboy, frightened by the endless artillery blasts, the moaning of countless wounded soldiers, and the stench of the First World War. He moans, audibly, the only prayer he can dare think of. "Oh, God." I've heard him and I have said, "Amen."

I hear him in the stillness of death—in an upstairs bedroom, a mourning father holding his lifeless infant, cuddling her, swaying gently, as if his rhythmic movement might bring about a miracle he barely has the faith to believe in. Through stifled tears he cries, "oh, God." I've heard him.

I'm not that good at praying.

Some days I write my prayers in a ninety-nine cent composition book.

Some days I sit and stare and do my best to contemplate—but my mind tends to wander and I find myself preoccupied by the mundane and by all that I think I have to do.

Some days I pretend to imitate Brother Lawrence and practice the presence of God.

Some days I read a missal that I once pulled from the trash and find that the Kyrie and Gloria lift my soul to a higher place.

Some days, as I wait for my children to fall asleep, I pray over them and for them in the stillness that the moonlight carries in through their bedroom window.

And some days I find myself thinking of that old photograph, of that man I never met, and I crawl to a closet, shut the door, and say what may be the most honest prayer I have ever prayed, "Oh, God." ❁

Some days, as I wait
for my children to fall asleep,
I pray over them
and for them in the stillness that
the moonlight carries in through
their bedroom window.
And some days I find myself
thinking of that old photograph,
of that man I never met,
and I crawl to a closet, shut the door,
and say what may be
the most honest prayer
I have ever prayed, "oh, God."

A number of years ago, I asked several friends in the music industry if they would write something on the subject of prayer that I could use for a music project I was working on. Nothing ever came of the project, but it did provide me with this short poem by Rich. I was at a get-together with some friends when Rich came up to me and said, "Oh, I've got your poem on prayer. Feel free to turn it into a lyric or just use it like it is. I think it would be good if you just read it in your really deep voice." I grabbed a pen and jotted down the words as he recited them. I later told him how great I thought it was, but he never mentioned it again.

I don't think Rich meant this to be some sort of definitive statement on prayer. The stark and despairing emotion it evokes should, of course, be balanced against other things that he wrote on prayer. Taken on its own, this is kind of a disturbing little poem. It isn't neat and tidy. It has claws. Of course, if you knew Rich, you would know that he was a person who liked to shake the rafters, and I think he's doing that here. BUT I THINK HE IS ALSO REMINDING US HOW EASILY WE CAN GET SO CAUGHT UP IN TRYING TO MAKE OUR PRAYERS BEAUTIFUL, THAT WE FAIL TO MAKE THEM TRUE. Often, the truest prayer is not polished and profound, but an inarticulate cry for help or a whisper of agony that arises from our pain. Perhaps those are the prayers that most touch God's heart.

*Jimmy Abegg*

DEAD ON ARRIVAL AT THREE A.M.
HEAVEN RECEIVED THE PARCEL I SENT
EMBALMED IN GRANDIOSE POETRY
BLOODLESS, LIFELESS, AND BEAUTIFULLY BOUND AND GAGGED
WELL MANICURED

THE PRAYER WAS LEFT...IT WAS NOT HEARD
BUT ROTTED THERE AMONG THE CHOICEST REPETITIONS
VAINLY VOICED, UNFELT, UNHEARD
THIS SAD ROUTINE...LAY DEAD
DEAD ON ARRIVAL AT THREE A.M.

TO GOD SUCH PRAYERS MUST SEEM THE MIRACLE OF MODERN ART
A STARVING MIND STRANGLING A HEART THAT'S NEARLY DRY
WHISPERING BARELY WISHFUL THOUGHTS
ITS LIPS CALL PRAYER...

*Some of these thoughts are echoed—perhaps with more hopefulness—in one of Rich's last songs, "Hard to Get." On the pages that follow, I've reproduced this song in Rich's own handwriting. It is no surprise that many consider it one of their favorite Rich Mullins songs.*
*—Jimmy*

1. You who live in heaven—hear the prayers of those of us who live on earth
who are afraid of being left by those we love and who get hardened by the hurt
... do you remember when you lived down here where we all scrape
to find the faith to ask for daily bread
did you forget about us after you had flown away
well, I memorized every word you said

Still I'm so scared (I'm holding my breath

while you're up there just playing hard to get

2. You who live in radiance—hear the prayers of those of us who live in skin
we have a love that's not as potent as yours was—but still we do love one another
did you ever know kindness — did you ever know how
do you (remember just how long a night can get
when you are barely holding on and your friends fell asleep
and you don't see the blood that's running in your sweat

Will those who mourn be left uncomforted

while you're up there just playing hard to get

I know You bore our sorrows ... I know You feel our pain

I know that it would not hurt any less even if it could be explained

I know that I am only lashing out at the One who loves me most

And after I have figured this, somehow all I really need to know

is if

---

## HARD TO GET

You who live in eternity hear the prayers of those of us who live in time

we can't see what's ahead and we cannot get free of what we've left behind

I'm reeling from these voices that keep screaming in my ears

all these words of shame and doubt, blame and regret

I can't see how You're leading me unless You've led me here

where I'm lost enough to let myself be led

and so You've been here all along I guess

and so it's just Your grace that gets me to just plain hard to get

MY LORD GOD, I HAVE NO IDEA WHERE I AM GOING. I DO NOT SEE THE ROAD AHEAD OF ME. I CANNOT KNOW FOR CERTAIN WHERE IT WILL END. NOR DO I REALLY KNOW MYSELF, AND THE FACT THAT I THINK THAT I AM FOLLOWING YOUR WILL DOES NOT MEAN THAT I AM ACTUALLY DOING SO. BUT I BELIEVE THAT THE DESIRE TO PLEASE YOU DOES IN FACT PLEASE YOU. AND I HOPE I HAVE THAT DESIRE IN ALL THAT I AM DOING. I HOPE THAT I WILL NEVER DO ANYTHING APART FROM THAT DESIRE. AND I KNOW THAT IF I DO THIS YOU WILL LEAD ME BY THE RIGHT ROAD THOUGH I MAY KNOW NOTHING ABOUT IT. THEREFORE WILL I TRUST YOU ALWAYS THOUGH I MAY SEEM TO BE LOST AND IN THE SHADOW OF DEATH. I WILL NOT FEAR, FOR YOU ARE EVER WITH ME, AND YOU WILL NEVER LEAVE ME TO FACE MY PERILS ALONE. **THOMAS MERTON, "THOUGHTS IN SOLITUDE"** ✸

"Give up trying to look like a saint," Brennan Manning's spiritual director once told him. "It'll be a lot better for everybody." If there is anything that the ragamuffins who contributed to this book have in common, it is this: They recognize that being a true follower of Christ is not a matter of polishing ourselves up to make ourselves more presentable to God, but of being honest about how far we fall short of being the persons we know we should be and reaching out to accept the freely given, wild and untamed, scandalous grace of God.

Perhaps no modern writer has more consistently and memorably emphasized this theme than Brennan Manning.

> *When I get honest, I admit I am a bundle of paradoxes. I believe and I doubt, I hope and I get discouraged, I love and I hate, I feel bad about feeling good, I feel guilty about not feeling guilty. I am trusting and suspicious. I am honest and I still play games. Aristotle said I am a rational animal; I say I am an angel with an incredible capacity for beer.*

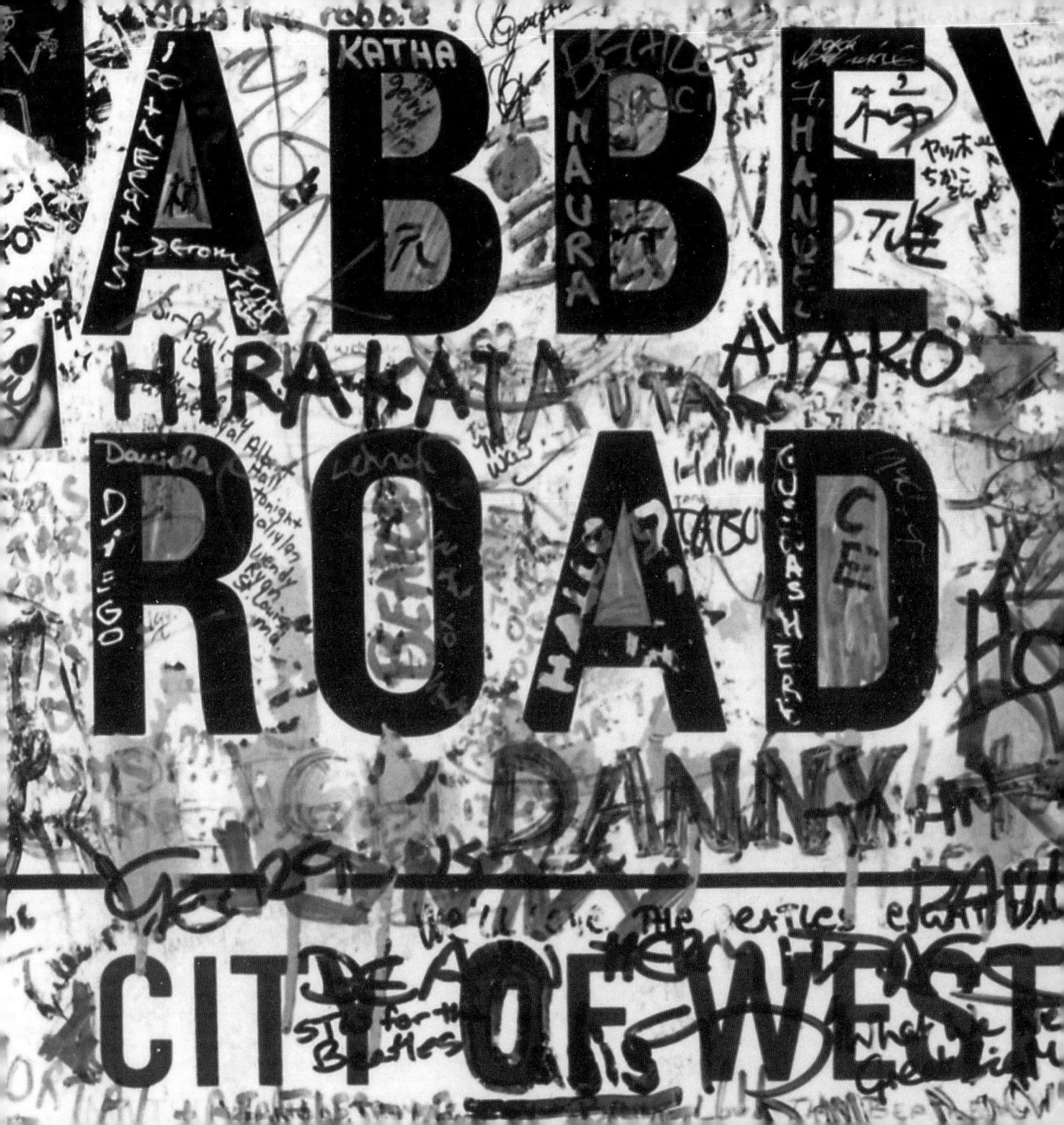
ABBEY
ROAD

*To live by grace means to acknowledge my whole life's story, the light side and the dark. In admitting my shadow side, I learn who I am and what God's grace means. As Thomas Merton put it, "A saint is not someone who is good but who experiences the goodness of God."* —THE RAGAMUFFIN GOSPEL

We can easily become so preoccupied with how others perceive us and with trying to perfectly model all the Christian virtues that we lose touch with the real message of the gospel, the good news that God loves us as we are, with all our failures and imperfections. And that God wants to have a relationship with us.

We can come as we are. His desire for us is not based on our performance. When we really grasp this truth, it will change the way we look at prayer.

*Let us suppose you give your three-year-old daughter a coloring book and a box of crayons for her birthday. The following day, with the proud smile only a little one can muster, she presents her first pictures for inspection. She has colored the sun black, the grass purple, and the sky green. In the lower right-hand corner, she has added woozy wonders of floating slabs of color and hovering rings: on the left, a panoply of colorful, carefree squiggles. You marvel at her bold strokes and intuit that her psyche is railing against its own cosmic puniness in the face of a big, ugly world. Later at the office, you share with your staff your daughter's first artistic effort and you make veiled references to the early work of van Gogh.*

*A little child cannot do a bad coloring; nor can a child of God do a bad prayer.* —THE RAGAMUFFIN GOSPEL

Contemplating this acceptance frees me to pray prayers that are honest and authentic; it gives me the freedom to express heavenward all that is inside me.

I recently spent three years immersing myself in a study of prayer. I read through most of the classic books on the subject. I grappled with the multitude of Scriptures that address the topic. I perused the current writings. I even prayed for better understanding of prayer. All this time spent was fruitful, and out of it I wrote a little book on prayer. But I'm no expert. I don't think I've even begun to scratch the surface of understanding the mysteries involved in our communication with God. And when it comes to practicing what I've learned, of actually giving prayer the place it deserves in my life and my time, well, let's just say that I'm glad that God accepts my looping scrawls of crayoned passion. I'm grateful that I don't always have to color inside the lines, because my hand and heart just don't seem to be steady enough.

Sometimes my prayers are carefully thought out, each word painstakingly chosen. Occasionally, in fact, I'll sit down and write out my prayers, trying to express as clearly as I can the depths of what is in my heart. I'll work and rework each phrase of my prayer, crafting it like a poem, trying to capture the rhythm of my soul's cries in the dance of the words, trying—always imperfectly—to make them say exactly what I mean, to capture precisely what I want to express to God. This has an amazing way of focusing my mind on what matters most. And the process of pouring out my heart on paper becomes a prayer in itself.

Most of the time, though, my prayers are less articulate. They arise out of the difficulties and struggles of my life— cries and groans filled with my pains and passions. They are not neat and tidy. They are not particularly religious. They are graffiti scrawled on the walls of heaven.

I've learned that anger and confusion and frustration can give rise to prayers that are every bit as real and precious to God as any of my more devout outpourings. The psalms are filled with moments when David stands before God shaking an accusing finger at perceived injustices or forming words that barely conceal his feeling of abandonment.

Like David, I don't have to hide from God all the thoughts and feelings that aren't very pretty. He is perfectly aware of what I am thinking and feeling anyway. Why would I need to try to cloak my emotions in pious terms? In the process of expressing myself freely and honestly, what usually happens is that I come to understand more clearly the real nature of what is happening in my heart and soul. Recently, frustrated with what seemed like God's silence in the face of great pain in my life, I found myself saying these words through clenched teeth: "God, if You want for us to have a relationship, You're going to have to keep up Your end of the deal." I don't think I managed to shock Him with this outburst. In fact, once it was spoken aloud, it helped me to begin to uncover some of the ways that I was trying to manipulate Him into changing my unpleasant circumstances. Trying to manipulate God, I have discovered, is probably not the best way of getting things done.

When it comes to prayer, I think we all feel inadequate. We spend a lot of time talking about praying, thinking about praying, or reading about praying. Sometimes we even spend time feeling guilty that we are not praying as much as we are convinced we should.

At times, it is sheer laziness that keeps me from praying. There are always other things to do: phone calls to make, things to read, people to see. Prayer is hard. And it is difficult to make time for things that are hard.

And sometimes, to be honest, prayer can feel irrelevant or hopelessly naïve. To pray can seem like the invocation of some sort of magic formula to try to get my way. Some people talk about prayer as though it is a system. I bring my needs and wants to God, hoping to persuade Him to do things my way because I've figured out how to "work the system." And then there is the question that haunts me a little: What should I pray about?—and what am I just supposed to be responsible for? I know that God calls me to be child-like, but I suspect that is something different from being childish. I don't want to ever fall into the habit of treating God like some sort of divine vending machine.

I'm learning, though, not to let my prayers be stifled by all these concerns. When I read the Old Testament I find it filled with examples of men and women who bargained with God. I think of Abraham, struggling to convince God not to destroy Sodom by haggling with all the skill of a used-car salesman. Or Jacob, wrestling with God and showing

BREAD

**Special**

EACH

QUALITY
& VALUE !

Full Line
of
Cold Cuts

KODAK

HOME
MADE

PURE

GROU

*Freshest*

*in*

himself unwilling to give up until he has extracted a blessing. The prayer lives of these patriarchs were more reminiscent of the wheeling and dealing of a middle—eastern street vendor than a polite and polished cleric. They give me hope that I can ask persistently, and even ask for the wrong things, knowing that God desires to hear my requests. One of Jesus' clearest teachings on prayer is that we should be bold to ask. That doesn't mean we'll always get what we want, but it does mean that the door is always open for our most heartfelt pleas to pass through.

I wonder if part of our problem in praying is that we have made prayer into something entirely unnatural, something that doesn't really fit into our lives. We burden ourselves with guilt about a problem we can't figure out how to overcome, when the answer may rest in merely changing our perceptions. Maybe if we grasped prayer as something more natural—less as a religious ritual and more as a real conversation—it would be easier to pray. Prayer is not about pious thoughts and words; it is not about postures, techniques, or methods. It is less a matter of quantity than passion.

Love is God's motivation for giving the gift of prayer. God values the scrawls I make on the wall of heaven because He values me. I do not pray primarily to get the things I think I need or to fulfill a religious duty. I pray because God loves me and desires to be involved in my life. I pray because, however imperfectly and unfaithfully, I love Him and I desire His companionship with me on the journey that is my life. Prayer is the most intimate activity I can share with God, the utmost in self-revelation, the place where I can bare my heart and soul before Him. In prayer I am made vulnerable to God, my truest self is revealed, and I find the promise that God is transforming this ragamuffin into royalty—a son of the King. ✸

JIMMY: It's great to have your participation in this book. I'm hoping an evocative portrait of what happens to people when they think about prayer will emerge from it. Your contribution is so important because you are someone who had such an influence on Rich Mullins and the Ragamuffin Band, as well as a number of these other artists and writers. I remember meeting you in Boston in about 1988 when I was playing with Charlie Peacock. We were doing a festival, and you were one of the speakers. I'd never heard of you, but the things you said that day really rang my bell. Next chance I got, I went out and bought your book *Lamb and Lion*. I loved it immediately. A few years later, I found myself playing in Rich's band. Eventually, Rich, influenced by your book *Ragamuffin Gospel* (which he gave me), decided to name the band A Ragamuffin Band. Over time, the influence of your book started a whole movement within our community of musicians, a movement that continues to take on a life of its own. Therefore, I guess I hold you responsible for the way we use "ragamuffin" to describe a certain approach to living out our Christian lives. Why do you think this word and this approach resonates so well with people?

church·        Port au Prince   Haiti

BRENNAN: I think it's because it is an accurate description of our real life situation, of the reality that we are radically dependent upon God for our next breath—that we can trust the God who has brought us this far and know He is going to get us through the rest of the journey. Of course, some have trivialized the term. Now there's even a muffin in a box called Rag-a-Muffin!

JIMMY: I think I saw that. It's a mix where you just add water...

BRENNAN: That's it. Yeah. . . but there are a number of reasons why the term works so well to describe our experience as followers of Christ. It is a way of seeing the Christian life that is different from traditional church culture. For example, ragamuffins don't get served, they serve. And when there is food on their plate they don't whine about the mystery meat or their distaste for veggies. They don't whimper about the cracked plate or criticize the menu. They are just grateful that their belly is full. Nor do they complain about the feeble preaching and boring worship at their church. They are just happy that they have a place to mingle with others who are also beggars hungering for God's mercy.

Ragamuffins are grateful for the Word, even though they may have read it many times and still know they haven't fully grasped the beauty of its message. The ragamuffin lifestyle is reflected in a simple wardrobe, unaffected speech, and a raw honesty about their predicament—which is their complete lack of power to achieve their greatest desires in life without God's help. Therefore, the ragamuffins are filled with gratitude for even the smallest gift. As ragamuffins make their way through the world, they have a sense of humor about the vanity of wanting to be noticed, of trying to be the center of attention. They know that the things of this world are passing away. Ragamuffins, by the way they live, testify to this truth. Ultimately, a ragamuffin is a prophet who prophesies without words.

JIMMY: This description reminds me a little of a book I've been reading called *Traveling Mercies*. I can't help but think that its author, Anne Lamott, would have been a great friend of Rich Mullins if they had ever met. Some of what she says sounds a lot like him. Here is this woman in her mid-forties who is trying to carve out a life of faith without all the usual church culture trappings. And paradoxically, she loves the little traditions that illuminate her experience in the church she attends. In one chapter of the book she asks a trusted spiritual friend about prayer. Her friend tells her that the two best prayers she knows are "Help me, help me, help me" and "Thank you, thank you, thank you." The simplicity of that is so lovely...

Brennan, you knew Rich Mullins pretty well, didn't you? I know he held you in very high esteem.

BRENNAN: Yes, I knew him pretty well. We talked often. Once I led him on a three-day silent retreat. It was a time of great vulnerability, a time when a lot of inner healing was going on.

JIMMY: Rich certainly wasn't a perfect guy. He had his rough edges.

BRENNAN: One of my favorite stories about Rich is how he got into a fierce shouting match with a woman and stormed out of her office. He was really hot. But the next morning, she woke up at seven o'clock to a buzzing sound outside. When she looked out the window, it was Rich—mowing her lawn. No words of apology—just an action.

JIMMY: That's great! When we did the *Homeless Man* film about him, it was amazing to see all the different sides of him reflected through his interaction with so many different kinds of people. His life was a tapestry. Each time we interviewed somebody else for the film, it was like a whole new chapter would be opened. I felt like I knew him very very well, but in fact, I discovered that I only knew a little portion...

Well, let's talk about prayer. What is your prayer life like?

BRENNAN: I basically spend an hour in the morning, praying over Scripture and then sitting in silence for about 40 minutes. At night, it's another 20 to 40 minutes. But my prayer is mostly this: Becoming aware of God's presence and listening…letting myself be loved.

JIMMY: Yeah, we need to learn to be quiet. In this day and age, there is just so much going on. It's easy to fill our lives with distractions.

BRENNAN: We seem to be out of touch with our feelings, especially men. We need to relearn that there's such a thing as a felt knowledge of God. This is a kind of knowledge that only comes when you allow yourself to become immersed in silence, letting Jesus seep into, saturate, permeate, and penetrate every part of you. It's one thing to do this cognitively. It's quite another to realize and experience it, to be in constant communion with it. That's where the silence is so invaluable.

JIMMY: That's the hunger, too. People are starving for real contact with God. And God is still incredibly active trying to find His sheep. I took the picture on the cover of this book when I was in England six or eight months ago. We were taking pictures in the countryside, and I wandered off and discovered this whole hillside covered with sheep. I was able to walk freely among them, and they didn't even seem afraid of me. The whole scene was so beautiful that I just roamed around and took pictures of the sheep. The one that adorns the cover has a kind of "caught in the headlights" look about him—a vulnerable, abandoned, faraway look. For some reason, I identified with him. We need to just stop and try to see what's off in the distance. To refocus our lives. To let God rescue us. What's waiting for us out there for each of us is the love of God…

Are you working on a book right now?

BRENNAN: Yes, I'm just getting started on the last chapter. It's called *Reckless Trust*.

JIMMY: Cool. You think there will eventually be a Reckless Trust Band?

BRENNAN: I don't know!

JIMMY: Any closing thoughts you'd like to share?

BRENNAN: Let me share a story…
Amid the breathtaking beauty of County Kerry in southwestern Ireland, Fionn MacCunhaill asked his followers, "What is the finest music in the world?"

"The cuckoo calling from a tree that's the highest in the hedge," cried his merry son.

"A good sound," said Fionn. "And Oscar," he asked another of his sons, "what is to your mind the finest of music?"

"The ring of the spear and shield," cried the stout lad.

"It's a good sound," said Fionn.

And the champions told their delight—the bellowing of a stag across the water, the baying of a tuneful pack herd in the distance, the song of a lark, the laughter of a gleeful girl, or the whisper of a wooed one.

"They are good sounds all," said Fionn.

"So tell us, chief, what do you think?"

"The music of what is happening," said the great Fionn, "is the finest music in the world."

JIMMY: Amen. ✸

JIMMY ABEGG *Ragamuffin Band, singer/songwriter, photographer, painter. (Nashville, Tennessee)* I'm told that I'm an unusual mix of creativity and gifts. I've managed to somehow practice a little of each, with a little help from my friends. Now I'll introduce you to my contributors…

CAROLYN ARENDS *Singer/songwriter, recording artist. (Vancouver, British Columbia)* I first met Carolyn on the "Brothers Keeper" tour with Rich. She's become a great friend. Her narrative style is charming and she's working on a book titled *Living the Questions.* She's from Canada so she sees things from a 'northern' perspective. Her music is wonderful too!

GARY CHAPMAN *Singer/songwriter, recording artist, television personality. (Franklin, Tennessee)* Gary has a unique life! He has been a great ally over the years as I have tried to do things slightly left of center. He's always encouraged me to aim high and try to see beyond the horizon. Plus, he's fun!

ASHLEY CLEVELAND *Singer/songwriter, Grammy winning recording artist. (Nashville, Tennessee)* She's got a big heart, and a big voice! Ashley is a remarkable talent and has great tales to tell! I can always count on an encouraging word from her (like me, slightly left of center).

BILLY CROCKETT *Singer/songwriter, recording artist. (Dallas, Texas)* Seems like a special angel lives in Billy's hands, because nobody plays the way he can. Again, someone who is trying to carve out a different path, and succeeding. We like the same painters too.

RICK ELIAS *Ragamuffin Band, producer, singer/songwriter, Nashville, Tennessee.* There's nothing like spending a day with Rick! He's an amazing mix of sinner and saint, a little rough around the edges with an inspiring creative intellect. He knows that he is loved. And he's got a lot more to say than he's willing to write!

TERRY GLASPEY *Author, speaker. (Eugene, Oregon)* New in my life this year, Terry brings a needed "middle" to all our "lefts" and "rights." He's been a keen observer of prayer for many years, and I think it's clear that God brought our lives together for this project.

PHIL KEAGGY *Singer/songwriter, recording artist. (Nashville, Tennessee)* Phil and I met when I was with Charlie Peacock. We relocated to Nashville at about the same time, and it's a pleasure to have watched his children and career grow during the ten years I've called him a friend.

PHIL MADEIRA *Singer/songwriter, recording artist. (Nashville, Tennessee)* Nobody makes me laugh harder than Phil! He has been God's gift to me over the years of reinvention in my life because of his vision for the arts. Amazing talent!

BRENNAN MANNING *Author, speaker. (New Orleans, Louisiana)* Brennan is the tether to which the name "Ragamuffin" is tied. God gave him gifts of grace, love, and mercy, and ever since he's been sharing them with others for years.

SARAH MASEN *Singer/songwriter, recording artist. (Nashville, Tennessee)* She's a fairy—no a sprite—no, it's sarah in flight! One of the most lovely voices in the world. She writes and sings in a different voice than the ones we're used to, and her gifts extend to every area of her life.

KEVIN MAX *Singer/songwriter, Grammy winning recording artist. (Nashville, Tennessee)* Our first book together, *At the Foot of Heaven,* was a fascinating experience. Imagine...poetry and paintings! We tried to push the envelope. Kevin has carved a pretty deep swath...a little left, a little right but mostly right down the middle of our culture.

RICH MULLINS *Singer/songwriter, visionary.* Rich made the snowball and set it rolling down the hill where it gathered more weight and girth until finally it rested at the bottom. We all began to add chunks of coal, carrots, a hat, and scarf. Now we can begin to see what it was he was seeing all along. He is sorely missed by all.

CHARLIE PEACOCK *Singer/songwriter, producer, and recording artist. (Nashville, Tennessee)* I met Charlie shortly after his friend with the saxophone prayed with him. Seems like we've been up and down every stretch of highway friends could ever expect to travel together...and lived to tell! Unknown to most, he plays amazing piano, and wow...can he fish!

BEN PEARSON *Photographer, filmmaker. (Nashville, Tennessee)* The closest thing to a soul brother I've ever had. We were cut from a similar patch of cloth, I'm sure. I don't think I would have taken a single photograph had I not met Ben, seen his work, and realized I should be using a camera. Of course he makes it look easy and his images are filled with heart—both qualities I may spend the rest of my life learning. Thanks, Ben!

MARK ROBERTSON *Ragamuffin Band, singer/songwriter. (Nashville, Tennessee)* I met Mark in Dallas, Texas while playing on my first Rich Mullins tour, pre-Ragamuffin Band. He was in Rick Elias' band. He was kind, very talented, and someone I could talk to for hours. Now we've spent years together, and I'm still not tired of his company.

BILLY SPRAGUE *Singer/songwriter, recording artist. (Nashville, Tennessee)* I've admired Billy's work for years and couldn't wait to invite him to contribute to this book. Its fun to watch him grow a new family and express his gifts in the way he does. He's writing a book called *Tell Me There's a Heaven.*

AARON SMITH *Ragamuffin Band, "Rock and Roll Hall of Fame" drummer (Nashville, Tennessee)* Aaron and I have been making music together since 1983! He's the real deal on drums! His style is to never brag, but I'm telling you that he's played with some of the all time greats. Plus he's a prayer warrior to boot.

MICHAEL W. SMITH *Singer/songwriter, Grammy winning recording artist. (Franklin, Tennessee)* Michael is one of those guys whose reputation precedes him, so I heard a lot about him before I ever met him. Now he's a trusted friend, and I believe God gave us each other to see contrast in lifestyle. He's into modern worship music as much as I am, and he gave me my first big break as a commercial photographer, so naturally he's special to me.

STEVE STOCKMAN *Author, pastor (Belfast, Northern Ireland)* I knew of Stocki's friendship with Rich Mullins, so when I first met him in Ireland in 1996, I sensed we had a long future together. He's been busy on the Internet, and in his part of the world he is a voice of sanity and reason.

BEAKER (DAVID STRAUSSER) *Writer, songwriter, photographer, painter. (Cincinnati, Ohio)* I met David about 1991. He reminded me of myself at his age, though nearly 10 years my junior. We went "right down to the river" philosophically and spiritually. So we've had our poles in the water ever since, watching the bobber for movement and hoping for a bite. David was a big influence on Rich's life and the co-author of many of my favorite songs in Rich's catalog.

MICHAEL YACONELLI *Author, pastor, speaker. (Yreka, California)* Mike used to write a magazine called the *Wittenburg Door.* That's when I met him. I was in a band called Vector, and he came to Sacramento to interview us. He has always threatened to start a church for people who don't like church. That's where I'm gonna go someday.

DESIGN: Christie Knubel & Karinne Caulkins/Jackson Design, Nashville
PRODUCTION MANAGEMENT: D. L. Rhodes/Jackson Design, Nashville

the beginning of a new legacy

# prayers of a ragamuffin
## (a ragamuffin band)

in stores now